206 (15) £3.00 BK

207

SIR TERRY FARRELL

BUCKINGHAM PALACE REDESIGNED

A RADICAL NEW APPROACH TO LONDON'S ROYAL PARKS

It is extraordinary how emotional people get about the idea of just taking the wall down. TF

ANDREAS PAPADAKIS PUBLISHER

Author's Note

This book was developed from ideas presented in *The Palace Redesigned*, a Channel 4 Television documentary screened on 2 January 2002. Sir Terry Farrell would like to thank David Barrie and Jeremy Bulger of Fulmar Productions for their vital role in this project.

Buckingham Palace Redesigned was put together by Eugene Dreyer and Jane Tobin at Terry Farrell & Partners in collaboration with Alexandra Papadakis.

Photographic Credits

All pictures are courtesy of Terry Farrell & Partners unless stated below:
front cover, 6-7, 8-9, 10, 16, 22: Aerofilms; 44-45: GMJ; 57 top: Charles Jencks; 32-33 top row, 50-51, 57 Alexandra Papadakis; 46-47, 59 bottom, 60-61 main picture: Andrew Putler; 20-21: The Royal Collection © 2002, Her Majesty Queen Elizabeth II

Front cover:
Terry Farrell's proposal to create more permeability for the Palace surrounds

Half title: Terry Farrell's proposal to open up Buckingham Palace

Frontis: Buckingham Palace was transformed into the people's palace for the Queen's Golden Jubilee celebrations 3-4 June, 2002

Title page: Existing and proposed views of the Buckingham Palace

Overleaf: Aerial view of the palace complex

Pages 8-9: View of Buckingham Palace and its relationship to the Royal Parks

Designed and produced by Alexandra Papadakis

First published in Great Britain in 2003 by

ANDREAS PAPADAKIS PUBLISHER

An imprint of New Architecture Group Limited

16 Grosvenor Place, London SW1X 7HH

ISBN 1 901092 40 2 HB

Printed and bound in Singapore

Contents

Architecturally it is not a great building; the composition is rather pompous. It is there to be added to and to evolve. TF

Foreword

Sir Terry Farrell

Royal parks and palaces play a vital role in the working of London. Specifically, they highlight the difference between the City of Westminster and the City of London, or the seat of government and monarchy on the one hand, and the seat of commerce on the other. These two sectors comprise the capital and they are as contrasting in urban plan as they are in function. Westminster evolved in an extraordinarily sub-urban, almost rural manner, while the City has its roots in the Roman fortified citadel. Together, they form the rather schizophrenic metropolis that is London.

The City of London is a typologically true European town. Roman in origin, it is planned around dense, gridded street patterns, a wall, gated entries and a high street (Cheapside). In the way that the Romans prescribed for their military purposes, the City is twenty minutes' walk from one side to the other. A truly urban form, its compact size made it ideal for banking purposes in the nineteenth and twentieth centuries, and practical for anti-terrorist barricades in the late twentieth and early twenty-first centuries.

Next to this tight form is the open, non-urban territory of the West End, which is based upon the random placing of four palaces (Buckingham, St James's, Kensington and Westminster) and six parks (Kensington Gardens, Hyde Park, Green Park, Buckingham Palace, St James's Park and Regent's Park). The main thesis here is that the royal palaces and their parks were built in the West End as anti-urban set pieces: they are great country houses set in rural parkland, originally intended as hunting grounds. Over the years, the parks have evolved and have become enmeshed and assimilated in the dense urban fabric. This shift occurred for two reasons: firstly, London expanded and enveloped the parks, and secondly, the monarchy has diminished and a democratic modern state has gradually grown in its place. Assimilating the royal parks into the urban plan was a significant part of the legacy of John Nash, under the championship of the Prince Regent. Nash's urban plans capitalise upon this encroachment, interweaving London's public areas within what was then the exclusive settings of the Royal Parks.

Out of the two arenas of power, it is the City of Westminster that has the true British character – after all, it is the seat of the government and monarchy. By some strange quirk of fate, the City of London has become purely a place of trade and commerce. In effect, as a specialised trading quarter lacking the diversity and heterogeneity of other urban districts, this Roman town never evolved into a true town. The actual integration of the City of Westminster and the City of London is still waiting to happen. The fusion of the two places cannot occur unless the City's view of itself shifts from being a purely trading centre to existing as part of London proper.

What are we left with today? The royal palaces and their parklands are the only public realm that we have in London. Far from being something that we are ashamed of, they present an opportunity for a glorious public realm. My concern is for their full integration into the fabric of London in a positive, creative and visionary way. The current failure to achieve this synthesis is to do with a lack of pedestrian access and a neglect to fully rationalise past changes. The focus on the parks needs to carry on beyond Nash's work. We need to integrate the royal palaces and their parklands once again. And we need to address the problem of the urban fabric between and beyond them. The result would be for the parks, palaces and city fabric to be planned as one entity. Currently, the parks are walled off from the palaces, the palaces are privatised and the surrounding urban fabric has problems of access and connectivity to the parks. The current situation does not acknowledge that the parks are anything other than largesse from royalty – a place where the public are occasionally allowed to walk.

The unique disconnection between the West End and the City is one reason for the shape of London's plan today. The other legacy is that handed down to us by Wren (in paper form) and Nash. These two great urban architects offer contrasting approaches to town planning in Britain. After the Great Fire, Wren tried to impose on the City an axial arrangement of grand boulevards like those found in the classically planned cities of Paris, Rome and Berlin. His plans failed because of the vested interests in privately owned, fragmented plots of land. Even in Wren's day, the City was not the centre of London – although it included St Paul's cathedral and the Port. It was the West End that was part of London proper.

Why did Nash succeed where Wren failed? Nash had two great advantages over Wren. The first is that he was building in the West End where there was less private and more public ownership, albeit in the shape of the monarch. This resulted in centralised holdings of land – a simpler form of land ownership than Wren had to contend with in the City. As a result, Nash – with the support of the Prince Regent – had the advantage of large landholdings and a major landowner as his client. The second reason for Nash's success is his partnership with the landscape gardener Humphry Repton. Together, they evolved an approach to town planning that was based upon British

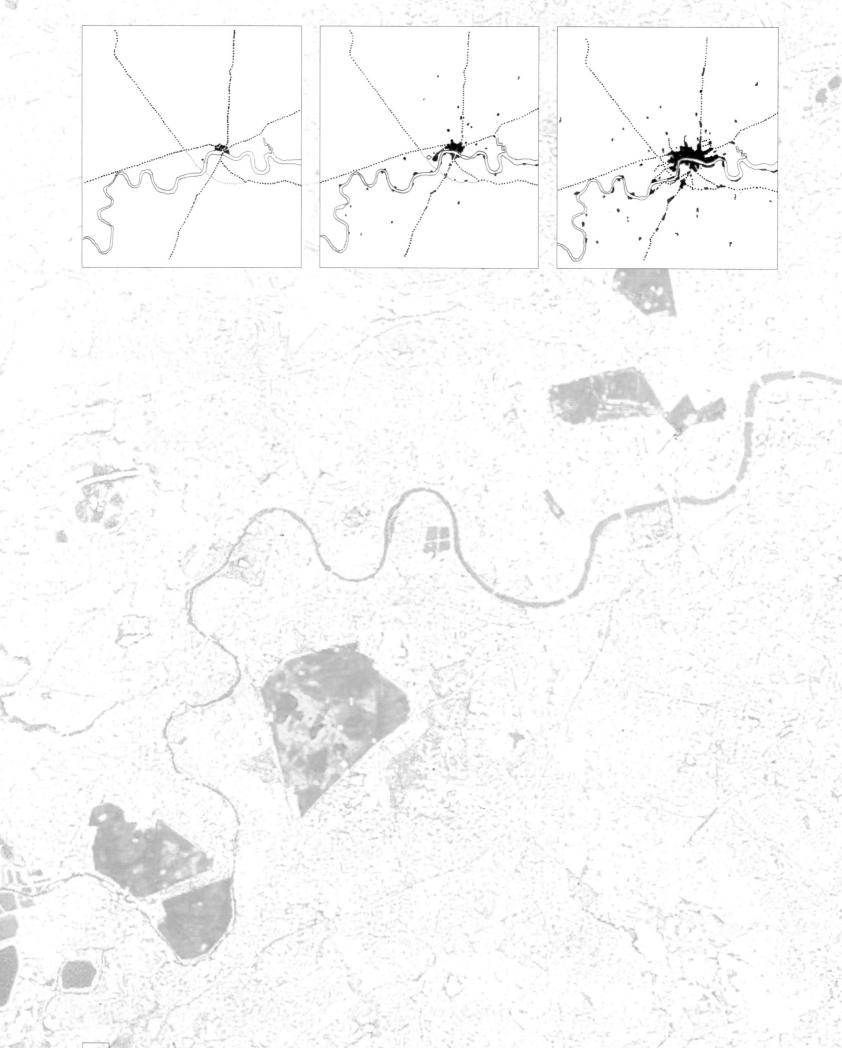

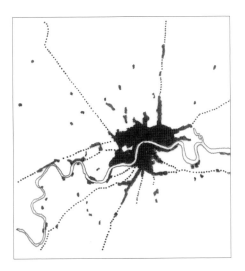  

Above from left to right: London's development from Roman times to the present
Opposite: The relationship of the Royal Parks – Regent's, Hyde, Green, St James's,
Greenwich, Richmond and Bushy – to the river Thames. Terry Farrell's strategy aims
to link the parks to form a joyous public realm

landscape design. The result is the development of the 'picturesque' approach to city planning. Repton's *Red Book* proved that the best landscape improvement schemes for the aristocracy's country estates adapted the garden design around the existing natural landscape of woodlands, lakes and hills. This 'picturesque' handling contradicted the convention introduced by the French, which completely reworked the landscape into a purely manmade, symmetrical environment of great boulevards and axes. Repton's 'picturesque' outlook was seized upon by Nash, who applied it brilliantly to town planning. The result is typified by Trafalgar Square, Regent Street and Regent's Park.

The 'picturesque' view invited an adaptable understanding of the urban terrain. Nash interpreted London's typography as a landscape around which the existing city could be built and adapted. The planning approach that Nash evolved was both realistic and pragmatic. Unlike Wren's scheme, which was rigidly *beaux-arts* classical and unfeasible in terms of land ownership, Nash's plans were effective and could be built.

The lesson to be learnt from this is vital in terms of possibilities for the royal parks today. We must continue Nash's tradition of the evolutionary picturesque approach to town planning if the parks and palaces are to evolve successfully into vibrant quarters of the city.

This leads to the often-neglected argument for the urban design of capital cities as a positive expression of governance – the urban theatre of affairs of state. Great capital cities use architecture and urban design to imply a strong organisational, governmental base for the city plan itself. This is self-evident in completely new cities such as Canberra, Washington or Brasilia – capital cities that were created as capital cities. In contrast, in historical cities such as Paris, Beijing, Berlin or Edinburgh, the seat of government evolved at the same time as the city itself grew. The great axis of Paris running from the old political centre of the palace of Versailles, through the Champs-Elysées to the Louvre is part of that city's urban identity. Similarly, the great axis and walls form part of the city plan of Beijing; and in Edinburgh the castle, the Royal Mile and Holyrood Palace are part of the city itself.

In London's West End – the heart of Empire as it was called a hundred years ago – the relationship between Buckingham Palace, Parliament Square and Trafalgar Square is key to understanding the expression of governance. Yet this layout is also an extraordinary misrepresentation. Buckingham Palace is

the grandest of all the buildings yet the elected head of state (who actually has more power than most, if not any, democratically elected head of state) – namely the British prime minister – lives is a small terraced house to the side of Parliament Square.

The implications of the three spaces, Buckingham Palace, Parliament Square and Trafalgar Square, are intriguing. Parliament Square, in the form of Westminster Abbey, symbolises the religious centre, while the Palace of Westminster symbolises the parliamentary centre. This is government and church united. Trafalgar Square – another unsatisfactory public space – is used for strangely controlled protests and gatherings. The third space in front of Buckingham Palace is where we gather to celebrate events of national importance: marriages, deaths, wartime victories and great national successes.

To paraphrase Winston Churchill, we form our places and our places form us. This is what is so fascinating about Buckingham Palace and its role in expressing the structure of the government that we have today. In many ways it is a complete misrepresentation of what is happening. This kind of misrepresentation has several problems. For one, it confuses the clarity of the democratic government to which we adhere. For example, when the American president wishes to make a declaration, he is conspicuously seen against the backdrop of the White House, driving through the great streets of Washington to the Capitol buildings. Writ large upon the streets of Washington, this journey makes a clear statement about the balance of power between the president, congress and the senate. In a similar way, Edinburgh's connection between the palace and the castle expresses a once-held view of how these institutions worked – the position of the new Scottish Parliament and its relationship to all of this has engendered considerable debate.

The British government as expressed by the urban form of London does not make a clear statement of relationships. If we make our places and our places make us, then we have to question who made the places and why and how they are remaking us. Is it right and do we accept that these places are making us? Architects must be involved in this debate, as well as in the ongoing evolution of the spaces and places within the public domain. This has to be done with humility, collaboration and confidence. I bring to the table the assertion that places do 'make' us. It is our responsibility to ensure that we agree with what it is that these places are making of us.

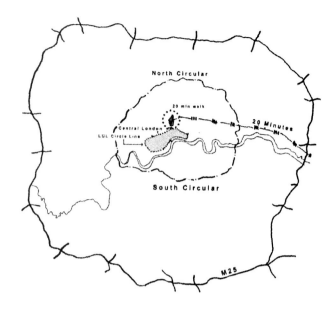

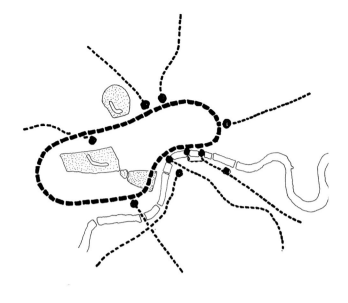

Above left: Diagram showing the relationship of the Underground
Circle Line to the central Royal Parks
Above right: London's transport infrastructure

Below: Contrast between Hong Kong's open spaces (left) and London's parkland
and (bottom) Hong Kong's built-up area and London's dispersed development
Opposite: Plans of London: The Roman city; Wren's scheme; London today

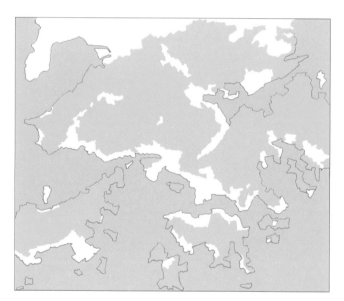

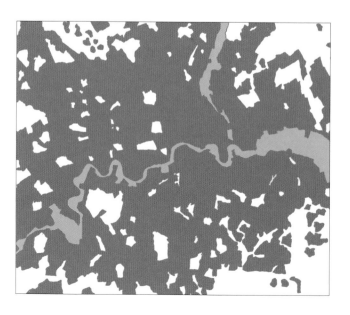

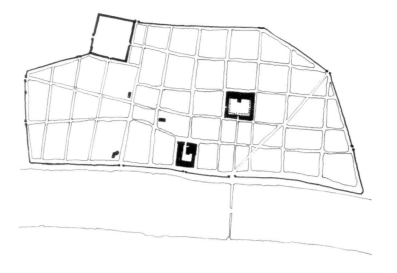

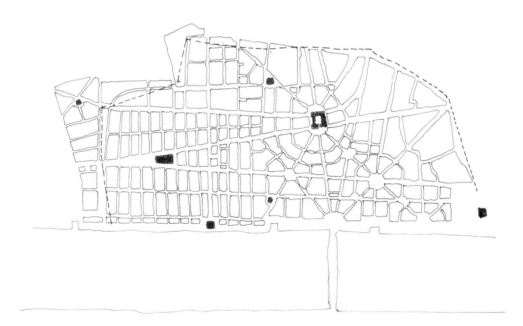

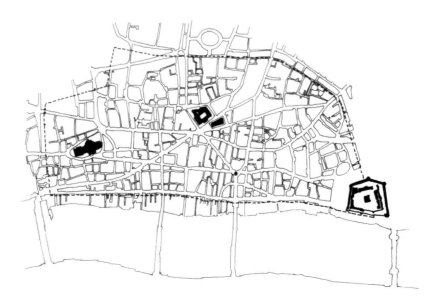

Buckingham Palace

300 Years of Design

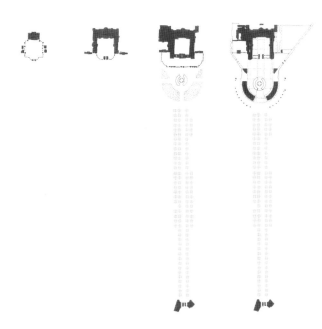

Above: Development of the palace, from its seventeenth-century origins as a private villa to the set piece it forms today
Left: The rear elevation of Buckingham Palace showing the Nash façade and courtyard, which have been masked from the front by Aston Webb's screen

Modifications to the design of Buckingham Palace span over three centuries and symbolise marked changes in the attitude of the monarchy towards the people during this time. The first house on the site was built in 1633; the Duke of Buckingham's Buckingham House was subsequently built in 1702–5. The house, situated between St James's Park and Hyde Park, was more of a country house on the edge of London than a house that capitalised on its urban setting – a precedent that is followed even today. George III acquired the property in 1761 and remodelled it as a private villa for the royal family, while the ceremonial court centre remained at St James's Palace. By 1826, George IV, with architect John Nash, had remodelled the existing private home into a palatial residence. The shells of the Duke of Buckingham's house and George III's villa are still incorporated within the structure of the palace today, dictating the plan, the room dimensions and the proportions of the ground floor.

Nash faced the exterior in Bath stone embellished with sculpted panels and trophies. He doubled the size of the main block by adding new rooms on the garden side. New wings were added to form a solid U-shape surrounding a courtyard enclosed by iron railings and a central triumphal arch commemorating the victories of Trafalgar and Waterloo (now referred to as Marble Arch and repositioned at the north-east corner of Hyde Park).

The next phase of remodelling was carried out for William IV by Edward Blore – at the time dubbed 'Blore the Bore' for his uninspiring work at the palace. Blore removed the picturesque element from Nash's design by solidifying it and taking away the dome and turrets from the roofline.

Queen Victoria moved to the newly renovated Buckingham Palace in 1837 but found it too small for her needs. Blore was again commissioned to design a new wing on the east side of the courtyard, thus forming a quadrangle. As a result, Marble Arch had to be moved to its current location at the top of Oxford Street. Blore's new front across the face of Nash's courtyard made no concession to the original architecture and consequently spoilt the unity of the palace. It also made it into a private, more introverted home. It was at this stage that the palace was closed off to the outside world.

When Edward VII came to the throne he commissioned the architect Aston Webb (in 1913) to create the imperial symbol that still stands today. Aston Webb refaced Blore's front (the original Caen stone had perished in the London climate) in Portland stone.

As part of a move to make the royal setting more ceremonial, King Edward commissioned a memorial to the British Empire in glorification of his mother's reign. This stands at the palace's front door, complete with ornate gilded gates and statues.

Today, the royal family live in private apartments on the north side of the palace; much of the ground floor and the south wing are occupied by household offices, while the principal rooms (the backdrop to court ceremonies and official entertaining) occupy the west block, facing the gardens. The building has not changed since Edward VII's time – when it was a symbol of empire.

Above left: View of Buckingham House from 1714. It did not become a palace until George III purchased it in 1775 as the official residence for the dowager Queen Charlotte
Above right: Part of an engraving by John Kip entitled 'A Prospect of the City of London, Westminster, and St James's Park', c. 1710. The image shows what are in effect two new towns (Westminster and the West End) on either side of St James's Park

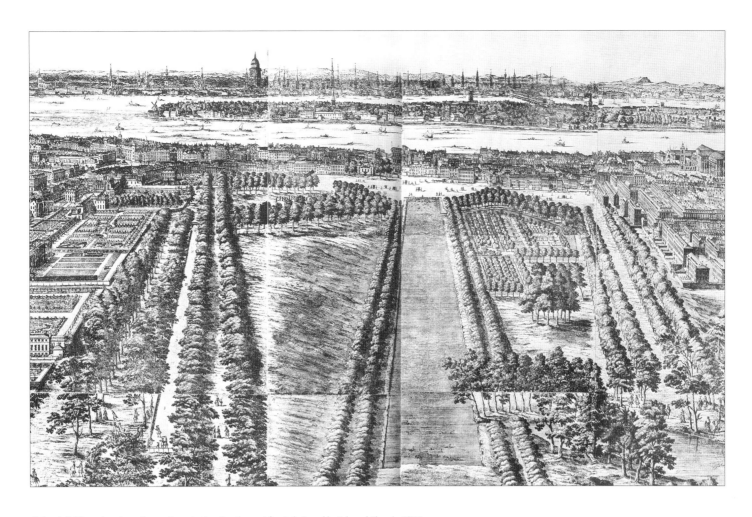

Below left: The palace from the south east, showing the east front designed by Edward Blore in 1847
Below right: The east façade, as completed by Aston Webb in 1913
Overleaf: Watercolour by Joseph Nash (1846) showing the east front from St James's Park. John Nash's Marble Arch is in situ
Page 22: The screen front has resulted in the palace becoming an enclosed compound. The Victoria Memorial
actually marks the site of a roundabout – a place for traffic rather than pedestrians

*Terry Farrell proposes to perforate the screen, opening up
the palace to form a joyous public space*

It is time to rethink the design of Buckingham Palace and how it relates to us today. For all its wedding cake finery, it is not the actual building that is a landmark of national importance – what should be the country's 'face to the world' that hosts its festivals and celebrations. The signifier is the urban setting: the sweeping circle (sadly a roundabout) around the Victoria monument, the gilded gates that lead nowhere (in a wonderful example of misplaced theatre, these gates are finer than the ones that lead into the palace itself), and the powerful juxtaposition of travelling from the imperialist monument that is Buckingham Palace to Hyde Park's slice of English countryside. Yet this setting is a piece of great urban theatre that is being played out without the full involvement of the British people. The whole set piece needs rearranging; it has evolved into a traffic interchange, giving more importance to cars than to pedestrians. Compared to Europe's wonderful paved squares and open spaces it is bleak and unwelcoming.

The palace itself should be opened up and transformed from its heavy, impermeable state. When it was completed less than a hundred years ago, it was designed to represent the scale and grandeur of an empire that no longer exists. The social and political conditions that created the great masterpieces of linked parks and palaces no longer prevail. Institutions are now required to be civic-minded and accountable. Somerset House – once a forbidding complex of government offices and now a wonderful public place – is a good example.

Ambivalence about the role of the royal family versus the rights of the public means that neither side gets the full benefit of these urban masterpieces. The monarchy as an institution needs to be shared with the people. Buckingham Palace and its park are part of a collection of urban forms that distinguish London from other cities; in world terms they are unique. No other city has its great palaces linked to parkland in this way and on this scale. Yet while the royal family barricades its gardens behind high walls, the experience for all is hesitatingly and incompletely revealed – the opposite intention of the original designs. The walls around Buckingham Palace gardens depress the urban scene for over a mile of central London. They are the epitome of thoughtless bad neighbourliness and characterise the palace as a series of signs that say 'Keep Out'.

The proposal presented here pricks the defensive bubble and once again opens up the palace and its park to the public gaze.

The Palace Redesigned

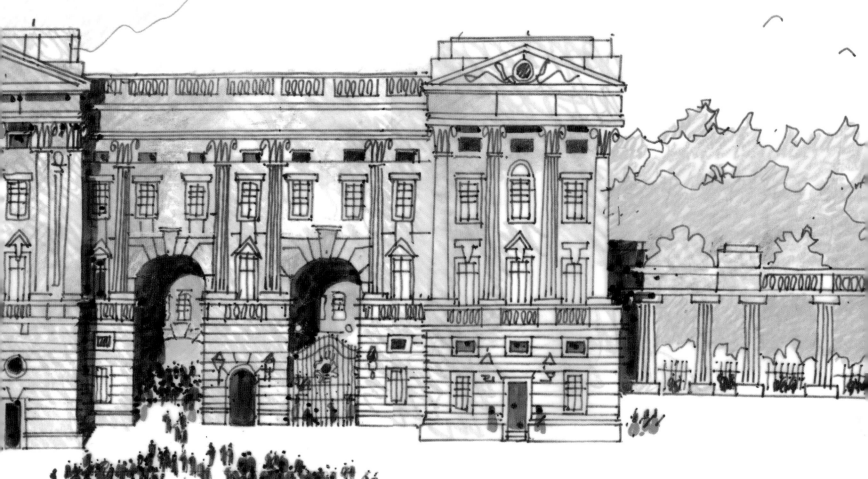

The intention is to build a radical new physical and emotional relationship between the palace and the people. The challenge is to humanise the area fronting the palace in order to create a more open relationship between it and the building. Perforating Aston Webb's screen wall with four arches would expose the hidden Nash courtyard, linking it with the public space in front of the palace. This extremely simple gesture would create a grand processional route. The facade of the palace would become a gateway, a transitional element that would take the visitor from the front space to the courtyard beyond; it would no longer be the barrier that it is now. The new square thus formed would be the grand gesture in a sequence of spaces that would allow people to walk down the Mall, through the square, through the old Nash courtyard and the palace itself and into the splendid gardens beyond. Like any owner of a great country house, the Queen could live in private quarters with all the tight security that she presently enjoys.

The urban improvements would continue with the perforation of the palace's garden walls with inset railings (like the enclosures around Brompton Cemetery) and gates, which would be just as secure as the present wall.

Buckingham Palace and its grounds would be integrated with the rest of central London and open for all to walk through (although they could be closed on special occasions for events such as royal garden parties).

The suggested drawings show a grand promenade from The Mall, up Constitution Hill, across Hyde Park Corner, through the Wellington Arch and Decimus Burton's screen, along Rotten Row to Kensington Palace. This route would be enlivened by events, pavilions, cafés and restaurants – similar to those found in Kew Gardens. With the walls encircling the palace gardens removed, Buckingham Palace, St James's Palace and Kensington Palace would be eighty per cent open to the public with exhibitions, galleries, museums, concert rooms, education and conference facilities inside the palaces themselves.

These plans reintegrate large areas of London, extending and building on the original designs. They suggest broad-scale schemes that should complement, but not be over-run by, day-to-day activities in the parks. Buckingham Palace is an essential part of London's urban design. It is only through such brave physical changes that the city can develop to embrace the needs of the new century.

The triumphalist façade presents a 'them and us' outlook that was fitting for the pre-World War I era when the palace was built. Today, buildings are becoming more accessible and open. They are required to be good neighbours to their surroundings

What are your thoughts on Buckingham Palace as it is today?
I like to think that you can psychoanalyse a building and see what it says about the institutions behind its walls. Buckingham Palace is not authoritarian: it is stiff, humourless, and Victorian in feeling, with all the worst aspects of the Victorian. It is a building that says that what is going on should be seen but not heard. There is no joy in what this institution represents or in what it says to the world about Britain. The whole presentation at the front is bad, as is the fact that you cannot readily stand around there (the tarmac is recent), that you are expected to keep moving and not stay in front; that it is a place of procession.

The front area used to be open. You could see into the palace as a great home. It does not feel like a house any more. It used to open its arms but once what I call 'the screen' was added, it took over the whole area in the front, so The Mall, right down to Trafalgar Square and Admiralty Arch, has been as it were colonised by this institution, by this Victorian vision of monarchy. It is not neighbourly; it is not good design; it does nothing for the parks and the public realm. It is far too grand, far too triumphalist. We need to revisit what it says, because in each century there has been a re-think about the relationship of the institution of monarchy with the people. Quite radical re-expressions have taken place and the present one captures the imperialist triumphalism of 1912 that lasted a very short time, not even until the World War II. I think that we are quite justified now in asking if this is the best front door for the monarchy or should it be re-examined?

Some people might say that it is symbolic of a powerful monarchy, that it is a substantial piece of architecture, that it
is a fitting emblem of power; that it is not a bad structure for the terminus of a procession.
There are many ingredients that almost work. We are a nation that used to have an empire and our history should not be jettisoned. The way the British succeeded over those centuries is a wonderful thing and is still there as part of our collective past. But Buckingham Palace was built at a time when perhaps imperial grandeur, perhaps triumphalism, perhaps a certain contempt for ordinary people was rife and so it does not encapsulate the right kind of feeling for today. It is almost too powerful, as clearly the monarchy does not run Britain from here. Britain is run down the road from a small house in Downing Street and from the Houses of Parliament, which have nothing like this pomposity. Nevertheless, the palace is there but it needs a more human face for today, a more accessible and open face. It is too monumental, too blank; it speaks at people not to people.

What about the façade, the screen?
My main feeling about the façade is that it goes against the original Nash concept of the early nineteenth century. In Nash's time, there was a wonderful arch – now at Marble Arch – and there was a courtyard that was open to the world. When they put the screen in front, and these tiny arches like little mouse holes, the composition was changed in a way that is disadvantageous to all the relationships, and so one idea we had – a very radical idea – was to put giant openings in the front to create a grand arched entrance rather like Nash's Marble Arch. I suggested two arches on either side – one in the middle would be far too much. But if you had two- or three-storey arches on either side, there would be penetration

Interview with Terry Farrell

The proposed scheme is both urban design and architecture, using the building to inject new life into what has become a moribund icon

through to the courtyard beyond. There could be some fine gates to make it secure but when the gates were shut you would still see through. What it means is that the Buckingham Palace façade – the wedding cake – would become a gateway. It would no longer be a cliff but a transition building leading from the front space to the courtyard beyond. That would be a quite extraordinary change of emphasis. I like it. People would see beyond it: they would still see the enclosure and they would still recognise the wedding cake that is on all the picture postcards. They would come expecting to see this iconic object, this plain and unexciting building and they would still recognise it but they would see it evolving. They would see a very literal change, a very physical, obvious change in how the monarchy relates to the people, how Buckingham Palace relates to the people. Now it says that there is no connection with the people, no connection between the private zone and public life. They would see it opening up; they would see a gateway that would be welcoming in the way that Nash's Marble Arch was before it was removed. I think that would be a terrific move.

What would you do with the balcony?
If I had the choice I would keep the balcony there. It was re-modelled in 1913 by Aston Webb but in fact the enclosure shown on the drawing was never built. I like that enclosure. He always had the balcony at the front, and the balcony itself is quite interesting: it is a family balcony, not a grand balcony or a dictator's balcony but a nice flat, wide balcony with a charming room behind it. What I really do not like about the façade are the wings on either side of it. But the balcony is a good thing and should remain.

You are talking about creating four new arches through the front. Are you confident about that? Are there any elements that bother you?
One of the most interesting things about the screen in front, which is relatively recent – less than a hundred years old – is that the palace hides behind it. Both gardens and buildings are much more delightful on the other side where you can see the doorways by John Nash and the entrances to the gardens. The screen is a Victorian statement about anonymity and about the period when it was built. The stone is a rather dull grey stone, whereas the stone on either side is a charming sandstone colour and you can see the trees on either side. But this thing in the middle is a big solid lump that is unattractive and does not say much to you about the occupants or the institution itself. I find it very dull and extraordinarily uncommunicative as a building.

The proposed arches through the screen are a fairly radical idea to many but the existing arches are really very small. There is an interesting view looking through the arches. You can see the palace and the forecourt, the dead space in front, and then the rather beautiful Nash building. You can see how the front pavilion is stuck onto a very fine more domestic residence at the back, with the gardens beyond. The problem is this pile at the front, this piece of grey wedding cake: instead of icing sugar it is grey and stolid like bread. I can see that putting large arches through the front may destroy some people's idea of the iconic object of the front of the palace but I do not believe in sitting back and not making any suggestions out of pure politeness. Architecturally, I have less inhibitions about it. It is not a great building: the composition is rather pompous and should evolve.

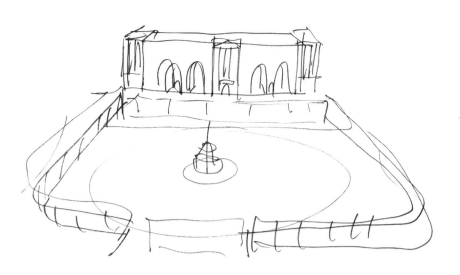

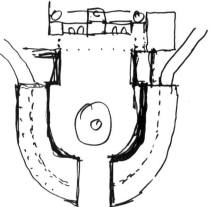

hockey stick shape?

Above: Sketches by Terry Farrell exploring the idea of the palace as a gateway
Opposite below: The Changing of the Guard is one of the world's greatest pieces
of urban theatre but bad layout and organization result in mayhem for the
general public who come to watch

What are your thoughts on how the palace will look?
I would like to explore how to make the wedding cake into a perforated gateway, something that you could go through to connect up with the great Palace behind, the magnificent garden behind, and so link the monarchy and the institutions it represents with the square in the front, which then connects with the world outside. So the arches would be like filters. It becomes a question of scale. There is a square on the garden side, a square on the Palace side, and there is a square on the public side. The existing front would thus become a link façade, a link gateway between the two realms. That is a great urban design device, a very familiar one, used as part of the architectural language in urban settings all over the world. A gate is a good symbol. A gate means a connection, whereas a wall means keep out.

Is there anything you are uncertain about?
The palace is an icon for people. They register it as part of the collective conscience and I feel very strongly that identification of who you are is part of where you are and what you recognise that place as. For the British people, Buckingham Palace is one of those objects.

One of the interesting things about the Palace is that it inspires people. When you go round it as a tourist all the attendants are extraordinarily helpful and really believe in what they are doing. There is an atmosphere on the tour that is quite exceptional and not like any other public historic building that I have been round.

Taxi drivers say to me that nobody should touch it. It is part of our life, our history, what we understand as our security. The British, particularly those of my generation, in recent times have locked into a feeling about security in terms of

their physical domain. Neither the French, for example, nor the Germans have anything like the same difficulty with moving on or adding to or evolving their physical domain in quite the same way as the British do.

You have not talked about architectural style. Why has this building been described as the white cliffs of Windsor?
It is an interesting expression. Buckingham Palace is clearly not a house. There is no front door; there are arches going through to something that is happening behind. At every window there are net curtains but there is no real evidence of occupation. It really is like a cliff. I call it a screen or a wall that has been placed in front of the house; the house itself is hidden behind the screen.

This is some kind of statement about the street, the space parading about the external face of monarchy as a thought-through public relations exercise rather than what they wanted monarchy to look like in 1912, and rather than what monarchy really is. Whatever the monarchy is doing behind there, you cannot see it any more. And in that sense it is a cliff, a screen: it cuts out communication; it is anti-communication; it is selling us something, selling us a story, selling us a concept; and it is not the right concept for today, if it ever was the right concept. There is a degree of hostility, of pompousness, of self-satisfaction and smugness that we know the British public and the monarchy, and we know the relationship between the two. I would like to take the best of it, develop it without throwing it away, penetrate through that screen, make this a public space, and make it all work by means of additions and re-interpretations that would retain the best of history. I think it could be sublime and I do not see any reason why not.

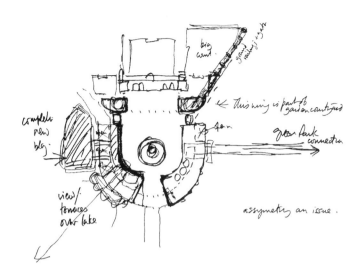

complete
new
bldg.

big
cunt.

grand
railings/reach

← this wing is part of
garden courtyard

40m

green park
connection

view/
terraces
over lake

assymetry an issue.

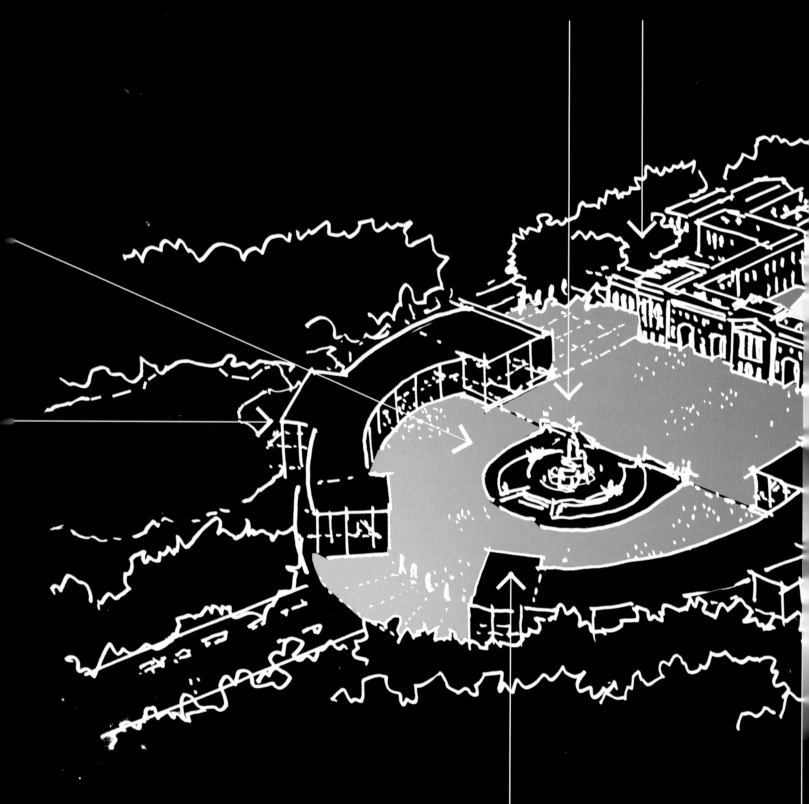

Outer part of new great square with retained Victoria Memorial fountains where all major national events to be held

2 The railing enclosed forecourt removed to create part of new great public square with direct access to central courtyard ("The Quadrangle"), Palace and gardens

3 The Aston Webb facade perforated by arches or colonnades to give direct access through the front building to the quadrangle

South Pavilion: an open colonnade connected to St James' Park with restaurant and tea rooms overhanging

7 North Pavilion: An open colonnade connected to Green Park

8 "The Quadrangle"- the courtyard to the original Palace now directly accessible

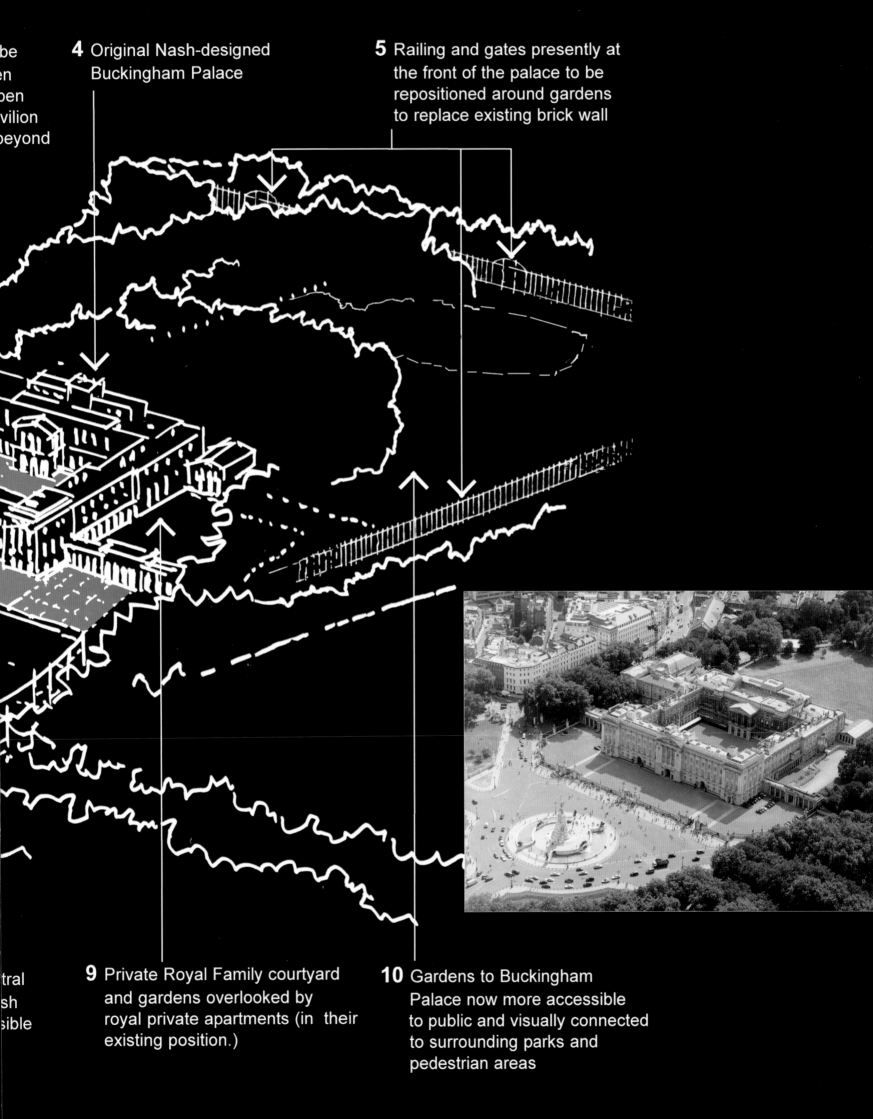

4 Original Nash-designed Buckingham Palace

5 Railing and gates presently at the front of the palace to be repositioned around gardens to replace existing brick wall

be
en
ben
vilion
beyond

tral
sh
sible

9 Private Royal Family courtyard and gardens overlooked by royal private apartments (in their existing position.)

10 Gardens to Buckingham Palace now more accessible to public and visually connected to surrounding parks and pedestrian areas

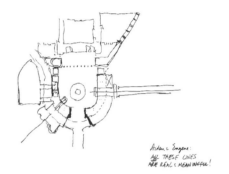

Above: Railings and walls form a domain that says
'keep out' to the world outside. It is a hostile attitude
that should now be reversed
Right: Terry Farrell's sketches outlining improvements
to the palace complex

How do you see the area in front of Buckingham Palace?
I like aerial photos because they show you more than a plan;
you can see things in three dimensions. When you look at an
aerial photograph of the area in front of the palace, it is
evident straightaway just how much of it consists of roads,
tarmac, and what I would call municipal gardens. The first task
would be to look at just how much available space there really
is. In fact, it is enormous and what is extraordinary is how much
of it is not of any real value.

What is absolutely extraordinary is crossing from this
great imperialist monument, this pile of masonry and
statues to a piece of the English countryside. It is an
incredible juxtaposition, a place of great theatre but the
theatre is not played out with the full involvement of the
British public. To see the Horse Guards in among the taxis
and cars is very strange. The tourists rush to see them and
people love the ceremony because it is real urban theatre,
and that feeling could be amplified. It would be nice to
have an explanation of who these soldiers are and what
their uniforms are, and why they are doing this. After all,
this is the place for all the great ceremonies, for weddings,
victory celebrations, and funerals; it is the public front
room, the main square of Britain. This is where all great
celebrations take place and I think we could make much
more of that in this century.

From the palace you see the parks in the distance but
look at the traffic, the number of cars that were not there
when the Victorians and Edwardians conceived of the
present arrangement. They had horses and carts: the motor
car had only just been invented. There was not the noise
and bustle of the traffic roundabout nor the speed, and in a
way they should not be there today. In the distance you still
have the glory of the park but the space in front of the
palace is bleak in comparison with some of the great
European squares with their wonderful paving. It has all
been arranged for the benefit of traffic and cars, not
people. There is some fine paving here and there, but by
and large it is not a pleasant place. Then there is the
strange juxtaposition between the triumphalism of the

enormous figure of the memorial and the little bits of
topiary here and lawn there, with scraps of flower beds. It
needs something more cohesive. It needs a greater sense of
purpose, and that purpose is that the public, pedestrians,
people who come and gather here should be given a clear
run of the place. This is their place next to the building that
for everyone symbolises the continuity of tradition and the
monarchy in Britain.

If the railings were taken down or re-positioned, the
space in front of the palace could become a very fine square
in its own right. It would be very radical but it is an
indication rather than a specific solution. If you then put
some degree of enclosure where the Victoria Memorial
Gardens are, you would have a fine public space. All this
would be very simple to achieve.

What do you mean by enclosure?
Now, when you stand where the monument is, you see all the
parks, buildings, and office buildings; everything intrudes into
the space. The Covent Garden Piazza has a great sense of
enclosure. It is a big space but the buildings around are of a nice
height. I am not necessarily proposing buildings in the solid
sense: they might be screens like the great Bernini screen in
front of St Peter's in Rome. There should be physical elements,
walls or columns, to make you feel that you are in a public
room. What I really like about the whole proposal is that you
begin to get a sequence of spaces: there is the courtyard inside
the palace, the smaller courtyards to the north and south, and
the garden then starts playing a part in the sequence. What you
would have is the traditional grand palace sequence of
movement from large spaces to medium to smaller, and out
again from smaller to medium to larger. That sequence through
the palace is the classic movement, which was lost in this
composition when the front pavilion was placed there. It still
exists in a glorious way at other palaces, at Hampton Court and
St James's. The sequences are not utilised but they are there and
not hidden as at Buckingham Palace.

What you have at Buckingham Palace at the moment is a
screen, a block with a monument in front of it and then wide

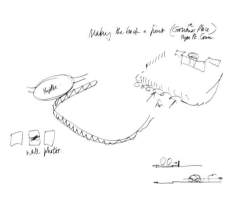

open spaces. It is not a place but a sea of tarmac, a sea of emptiness; agoraphobiasville. My feeling is that you should start putting things around it as Aston Webb originally intended: screens, pavilions, garden architecture. Once you have a place, people will come to it and be more settled. They will be able to walk about; it should be car free and not only car free but as car noise free as possible. It is not an oasis because it is a place where the public will come in large numbers as they do now. The railings could be pushed back quite a bit to have greenery behind them rather than tarmac, which speaks of military processions and parades that are not very meaningful today; or they could be replaced with gates so that people could walk in at certain times of the year. You could even rail off the whole space. A spatial enclosure would provide heightened security and the whole experience would be much richer, much more varied. There could be more festivals, more celebrations there, and when there is a great event people could come up to the railings. At the moment they are kept too far away.

People should be allowed nearer?
Yes. When the royal coach approaches or the Royal Family comes out on the balcony, people rush to the railings. I find that quite a strange gesture today. It is as if they are paupers at the gate. It is the wrong kind of relationship. The railings are excessive. They are symbolic, ceremonial railings that are not there primarily for security. They are meant to say something and they say the wrong thing.

What does not work?
Take the Kennedy Gate, which looks into Green Park. It is only there for theatrical effect, to give an imperialist scale to the space on the other side. It does not lead anywhere. It says 'pomposity,' 'grandeur,' and it contains the other side in a way that makes it seem bigger, more imperialist, more triumphalist. It is a fine piece of gate but a fake piece of urbanism. It is imposed upon the park, and destroys the relationship of that space with the park, which could be much more glorious. I would love to come down this route from Piccadilly and enter a fine square that people would enjoy in a more positive way rather than finding these containing gates and railings that are not at all the right thing for a public space, for accessibility and openness. They give completely the wrong message.

Another example is the contrast between Green Park, which is wonderful and, on the other side of the low wall, the Queen Victoria Memorial Gardens. They occupy a large area but are suburban in feel, with small, low plants. The layout is municipal and on the wrong kind of scale. There is more space given to the lawn and the bits of shrubbery than there is for the public to stand in. And then there is a very busy road, several lanes wide, and then the public area. It is all a a bit of a mish-mash really, not a fine space. Is it a roundabout, is it a bit of a public space, or is it a garden? No one seems to have thought through what it means, and yet for most British people it is the most important public space in Britain. It is the place where we go as a nation to celebrate when we have won a war, when there is a funeral, when we have won the World Cup. I would like to see a more animated space. I would like to see the Queen's Christmas broadcast on a large screen here. I would like the space to be more beautifully and simply designed with a greater sense of purpose, so that we know what to do with it. What it says now is that we do not know what to do with it. And that is the issue.

Looking down The Mall there is another anomaly. There are two pairs of gates but neither goes anywhere. They are there just to create a grandiose symmetry. It as though the occupants wanted to make it seem as though they were ruling the world from here, but it all has a hollowness to it because the routes do not go anywhere. It is purely a stage set and it is a poor piece of design by urban design standards in comparison with other great spaces such as the grand Parisian squares. Even smaller towns like Krakow in Poland have wonderful public squares. In my view the one in front of the palace is poor quality and poor in inspiration. It may have great gates and great figures but they are put together in a way that does not work. They totally lack the right imagination and the right character.

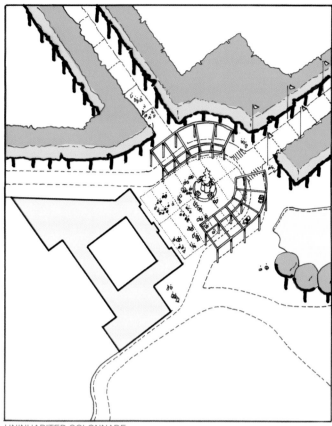

UNINHABITED COLONNADE

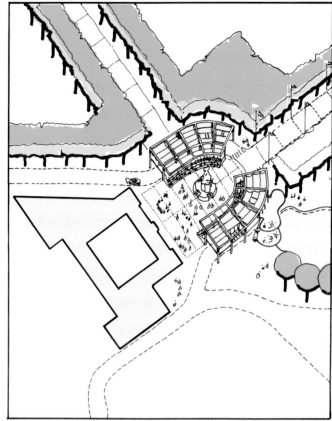

INHABITED COLONNADE

1. Collapsible seating stored below ground
2. Service modules: toilets, power, lighting and ancillary backup
3. Spectator and commentary boxes
4. Colonnade with traffic route to rear
5. Lightweight colonnade
6. New public square
7. Pavillions in Park - restaurants etc.

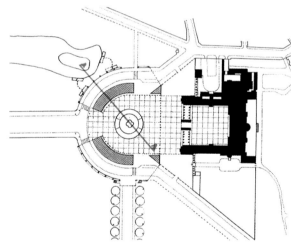

St. James Park   New Colonnade   Victoria Fountain

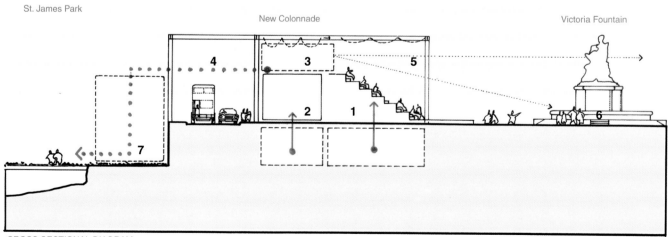

CROSS SECTIONAL DIAGRAM

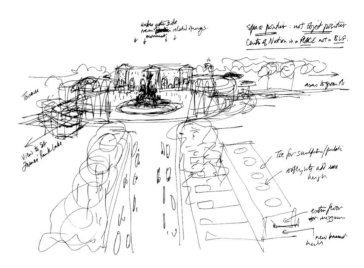

Above: A good precedent is the courtyard at Somerset House revamped by Jeremy Dixon:Edward Jones in 2000. The new scheme transformed the area previously used as a car park into a public space incorporating a glorious fountain display. In winter, the space comes alive as a highly popular skating ring
Right: Terry Farrell's ideas exploit The Mall as a grand processional route leading to a new square. The vista would lead to the palace and culminate in the gardens beyond
Opposite: Terry Farrell's proposals exploit the area around the Victoria Memorial as a place for gatherings and national celebrations. The design is based on a simple colonnade around a new public square

When you look at some of the things you are thinking about, can you picture the changes already?
We do not have a great tradition in Britain of squares and multipurpose public spaces that might be civic. What I would like to see here is a square of ceremonial and civic national importance. There is a role in every city, in every country, for different types of public spaces and this square could be a place that is yet to be invented in its pole role. Everyone should contribute to the idea of its use. If you make a public place, it is not for the architect or the planner to say how it will be used. The formal routes, processional routes along Constitution Hill are fully accessible. They are the great routes that we all know, that we see as such on television but we should remember that the routes are not fixed and could change. They would not be significantly altered, and I believe would be enhanced by a square in the middle. By a square I mean a place with a degree of enclosure, a good, reasonably hard, flexible surface; a space that is pedestrianised for most of the time but it could have traffic at times, and great processions could enter it and go on through the arches. Ceremonies of national significance – the Changing of the Guard, the great processions to and from the Opening of Parliament, weddings, funerals – could take place here with all the glory and pageantry they have now. The great strength of successful public squares is that they are highly flexible but also somewhat specialised. There are magnificent squares on the Continent: the square in Siena has a range of uses – even horse racing, although I am not suggesting horse races here. St Mark's Square is very much more formal without all the tourist tat of other squares in Venice. Then there is the wonderful new square at Somerset House: it has ice rinks; it has concerts; it has its own civic role, its own character. The new square I am proposing in front of Buckingham Palace would have its own character because of the parks, because of the

great processional routes and particularly because of the symbolism of the palace. The ceremony would continue but there would be new things too.

It would be a place of pageantry but ordinary things would happen there too?
To say that the pageantry would disappear or be diluted because people have more access to it, is degrading. At the moment you see people rush to the railings and so the pageantry is between giants and mice. That is an exaggerated statement of what and who we are. We should have great pageantry without that artificial grandeur and diminution. For example in front of St Peter's in Rome there is that wonderful colonnade and the great cathedral all created by far greater artists and architects than at Buckingham Palace, but it is a place of very significant ceremony with its own pageantry and in the same way the square in front of the palace could also have its own pageantry.

Buckingham Palace is always seen in this setting. You do not see it close to. There are many other buildings in the world like it, but it is the setting that tells you that it is Buckingham Palace, not the actual building itself but the Victoria Memorial, the big circle, the extraordinary gates that do not go anywhere, with all their gilt and black. There is also the suburban lawn that sweeps round occupying probably half the total space, and the traffic going round and round. Is it a roundabout? Is it part of the London road system? Is it a great pedestrian space? Is it a garden? It cannot make up its mind, and at that level it fails. It could be so much more successful. All the ingredients are there. With some added elements, it could be an extraordinary space, the finest public room in Britain where we all come together much more naturally than in the false settings that have happened over time.

Above and right: Before and after views demonstrating the revitalising effect that opening up the palace walls would have on the surrounding area
Opposite: Terry Farrell envisages creating for Buckingham Palace gardens perforated walls similar to those around Brompton Cemetery

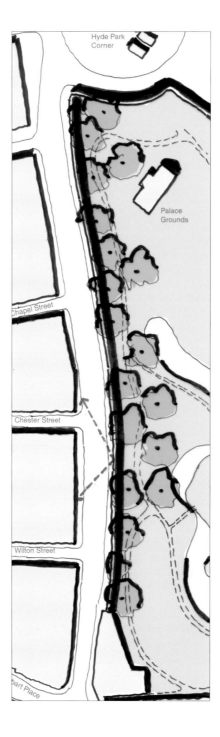

Hyde Park Corner

Palace Grounds

Chapel Street

Chester Street

Wilton Street

bart Place

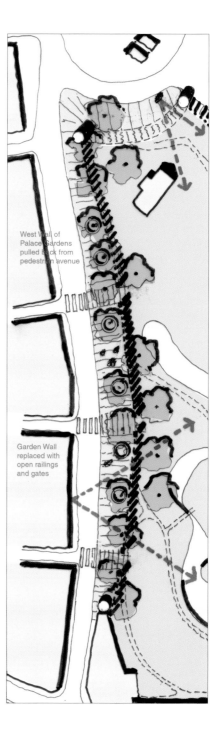

West Wall of Palace Gardens pulled back from pedestrian avenue

Garden Wall replaced with open railings and gates

OPENING THE WALLS TO BUCKINGHAM PALACE · T·FARRELL·99·

When you look at the gardens of Buckingham Palace do you want to occupy them? Is that part of your moral drive?

The gardens of Buckingham Palace are huge. When I have discussed with people the idea of bringing them into the public realm some have said that it is really a private garden, that you cannot occupy it; that you cannot go in there with hamburger stalls; but that is not what I mean. I think that that wonderful space could add to the richness and experience of London in many different ways. I like the fact that it is a private garden and that it is tucked away but to go in there, into a secret, private garden some of the time, perhaps just at weekends, perhaps just on feast days, and to have views into it in certain areas and from certain vantage points would enhance London. I am not really on a crusade to take over the garden. I am saying that it could do a lot more for London and thus a lot more for the Royal Family. I think that they are just as much walled in as we are walled out because there is a wall right round the gardens. It is a garden wall, a back garden wall. It is the kind of wall you would expect around a house that you are trying to keep neighbours and intruders out of, not a wall next to the wonderful setting of Green Park, the wonderful walkways to Hyde Park, a public domain that is sublime, the best bit of London. And here is a back garden wall. But it was not always so. This was common ground when it was Buckingham House. I am not sure when the wall was built – nobody is – but it is a wall that was clearly an expedient thing, with spikes on top, and barbed wire on top of the spikes. There are speakers and surveillance cameras. It says that the inmates are under threat and we are to be kept out. It says nothing about neighbourliness. And yet on the other side of the wall are forty acres of fine garden with two thousand different species. It is not parkland but a genuine garden. It has lakes, it used to have flamingos. It was laid out by Humphrey Repton, the great landscape architect who was a contemporary of Nash, who designed the palace. So there is something quite wonderful in there, but we have no view of it because of this hostile blank wall that goes on for nearly a mile around the whole garden, hiding it from our view and making it inaccessible. If there were railings, and if we could see in, we would see something wonderful.

Are you angry about the walls?

Yes. The trouble with the Royal Family is that it is a double bind. As with any idealised family, you want them to look after you and you want to be respectful and generous-spirited to them. But it is not like that any more. With a wall like this there is no sharing. It is bad neighbourliness and it sends out the wrong message. Either they are paternal and they share in a paternal way and we enjoy it; or they are behind walls, and it is us and them. Unfortunately at the moment it is us and them, and so neither side wins.

What would you do about the wall?

The boundaries are a long way from the edges of the gardens. If the first railings were perhaps 10-15 metres back from the walls, you could then generously landscape that area, particularly along Grosvenor Place and towards Victoria. It would be a gift to the street where now there is an unrelieved wall and heavy traffic. Recessing the new enclosure would give a landscape element. It could be called the Victoria Memorial Gardens and replace the suburban garden that would be lost in front of the palace. There could also be occasional gates so that when the palace gardens are opened in the future, people could come in from the street quite informally. Gates would give flexibility and would begin to structure the enclosing railings, begin to give vistas. Gates are wonderful things to look through. A fine gate frames a view. If there were gates in railings, it would be much more magical than the existing dull wall. It would add to the experience of London. It would not threaten the security of anyone inside. It would just enhance all our lives. Another point is that the garden façade here is extraordinarily asymmetrical. There is a lot of garden towards Hyde Park Corner and the private garden of the palace is next to the house itself. Many of the walks and the dense woodland where I suggest the railings be positioned are a long way from the house itself and so private areas and less private areas would be separate, and the plan might work quite well.

Should the gardens be public gardens?

In my view the gardens should not opened to the public in a general way – in fact they are now open in summer as part of the tour. But to open them visually would do a lot more. Now the wall is unrelieved, blank, and hostile whereas railings could very readily and very easily speak volumes about our relationship with the monarchy, and would create an urban landscape that we could all share. It is within the gift of the palace, of all the institutions that control these things, to change this at very, very little cost. With a bit of thought and a change of attitude we could have something quite superb. That is the main thrust of my argument.

Terry Farrell & Partners' earlier masterplan scheme reinstating public accessibility to St James's, Green and Buckingham Palace Parks
Key to public areas:
A. Hyde Park Corner and Constitution Arch
B. Buckingham Palace
C. Victoria Memorial and The Mall
D. St James's Palace
E. Carlton House Terrace and Pall Mall

Seven-point plan to reinstate public connections to Constitution Hill and Buckingham Palace Park:
1. New pedestrian crossings linking Hyde Park to Constitution Hill
2. New boundary railings and gates to replace existing 3-metre high wall
3. New fence and gates in Grosvenor Place (gates located to correlate with street ends)
4. New pedestrian crossings linking Green Park to Buckingham Palace Park via new gates
5. New main gate of palace forecourt
6. Remove existing 3-metre high garden walls and improve links to The Mall from St James's Palace
7. Bring ground-level colonnade into public use as cafés, shops and museums

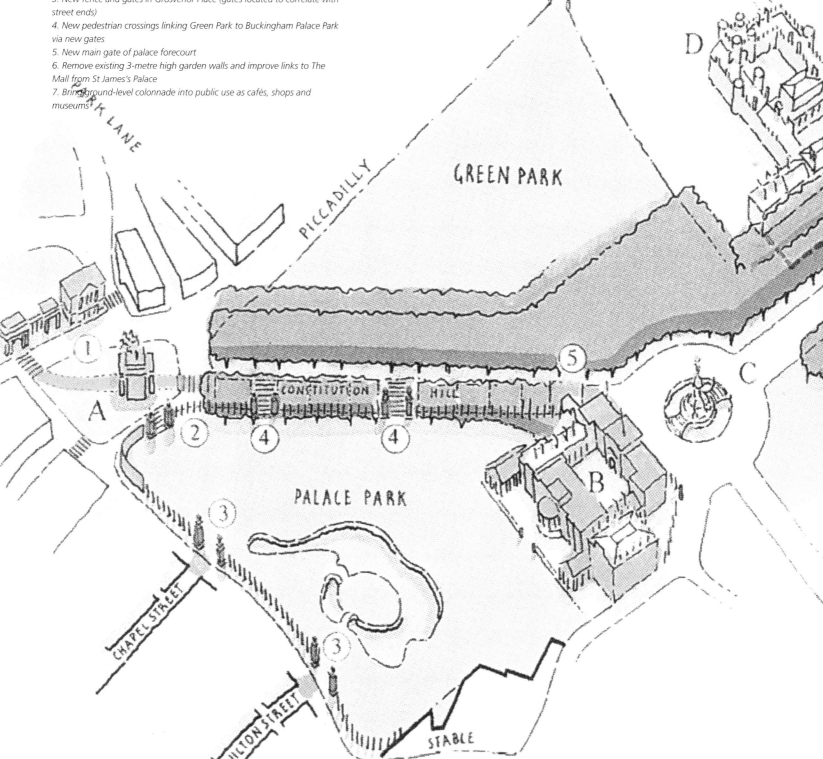

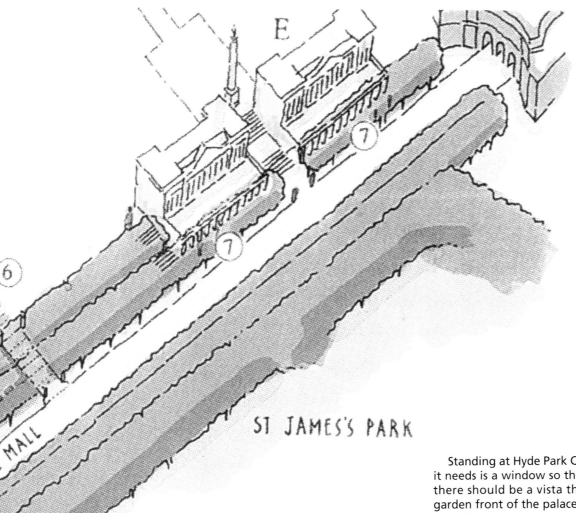

E

⑦

⑦

⑥

ST JAMES'S PARK

E MALL

How is Buckingham Palace linked to the Royal Parks?
Hyde Park Corner is the hub that links all the royal parks: it links the palace frontage, St James's Park, Green Park and Horse Guards on one side; and across Hyde Park to Kensington Gardens on the other. From the top of the Wellington Arch you can see right across the gardens of Buckingham Palace, a glorious view of lovely gardens. However, the wall around the palace is much higher there than around the rest of the gardens. In other words, if the wall was not there it would be possible to link the views of three parks to a wonderful view of the palace gardens.

Cities are about linkages, connections. People come together in cities because they interact, they meet there. Vistas and visual connections are a very critical part of that experience. And to be in a key hub like Hyde Park Corner and to understand the terrain, to understand why Buckingham Palace is in that direction, that there is a garden, that the front is round the other side, and to have the visual connection of this critical hub between the great parks at the Wellington Arch on a key route, on a processional route, allows us to make the kind of connections that everyone understands that cities are about. And that is why vistas, good landscape, and visual connections let you read the city in the way it should be read: you are reading the connections between institutions, between spaces, between routes. Here we have a strange part of London that is wonderfully open and strangely closed. The whole experience would be improved if more of it was opened up with windows into those other worlds. London would be enriched in the process.

Standing at Hyde Park Corner, I suddenly realised that what it needs is a window so that instead of the railings and gates there should be a vista through to the lake, the wonderful garden front of the palace by Nash, and the Royal Mews. You would be able to look through there at ground level and have the view to or from The Mall that you now have only from the top of the Wellington arch.

What is surprising about Hyde Park Corner is that it is mounded at the top end. It is a wonderful place to stand and look back down Constitution Hill and up the long avenue through Hyde Park. To add to that a southern view looking through a new window, a very formal window, possibly a big haha – instead of railings and walls you could have a haha at a kind of defended line that went down instead of up – would be a quite extraordinary thing to have on this great pedestrian processional route. In fact there are several overlapping pedestrian routes: there are the State ones, but there is also the route from St James's to Green Park with occasional views into Buckingham Palace gardens, and then across the junction to Hyde Park. That would give the maximum amount of delight and connectedness. That is a new idea, and one that I like!

Basically you are making the assumption that the walls should come down and railings be put up?
No. I am not making any assumptions at all. I am asking people to think about these things. I think you could mix and match. You might do nothing but make that window, and if you did just that, I think it would be rather a sublime and wonderful thing for London. I am not suggesting that any or all of this is critical or essential. I am merely making suggestions for people to discuss and talk about and if just one part of it is thought to be a good idea then it is worthwhile. The window could exist independently. One might also think about the railings independently, but in my view it would be better to think collectively. I would just like to argue in favour of it and to persuade people to think about these things.

What about the Royal Parks themselves?
The parks are now in the public domain; they are the public's parks, but they are the remnants of the old Royal Parks and the most glorious bit of London. They are absolutely astonishing. Pieces of trapped countryside in the middle of the world's largest metropolis. And to find the countryside here is a great, great delight and a great asset to London. But they are manmade in the sense that all these institutions of palaces and walls and buildings have been added to them.

The palaces, their gardens and St. James's Park were all part of one urban landscape set piece. Wonderful, great achievements. But when the park became public in our age of accessible democracy, and the lands behind the walls were retained by the royals, then the division began.

What was really extraordinary about the original design by great architects and great landscape designers was the sequence. I would love that sequence to be accessible again. I do not know what happens in the gardens of Buckingham Palace; none of us knows; but I suspect that they are not always fully used. We all know that the Royal Family does not live in London a lot of the time. So the real loss is that we cannot enjoy the splendours of the palaces and the gardens in the way their designers, their builders, their creators originally intended. It is a loss that we could rediscover without having to go back on a lot of the traditions of today. If it were all opened up we would discover great splendours that are found in no other city in the world.

What about the processional routes?
The Mall is one of the great processional routes if not the great processional route of Britain. It is one set piece from Admiralty Arch to the Palace. The square and the arch are designed by the same architect. The wide avenue from Buckingham Palace to Admiralty Arch is not only used by royalty: the London Marathon finishes there and Christmas events take place there. It is a great public gathering space, and really the only formal avenue of its kind in Britain. It is the kind of thing you find all over Paris, and in parts of Berlin and

parts of Rome, but this is the only one in London. It is a very fine one but it is layered onto quite an interesting and complex history because there are private palaces and great houses all down one side. And the park, St. James's Park, was an extension of those palaces.

We all remember this point as being where the funeral procession of Princess Diana stopped and the men of the family including her sons joined the cortege and went down to Westminster Abbey. They came out of St. James's Palace but it was not evident that it was St. James's Palace because the connection between St. James's Palace and The Mall is weak. It would have been stronger once but now there is no gate and so they came down this side street to join the procession. That was a moving use of the urban theatre of London. On such occasions the great parks, the great monuments, and the great palaces are an asset to the nation. The rest of the time The Mall is a fine avenue with beautiful walks, but the walls and what happens behind them could do much more for us. And it is really quite deplorable the way some of the assets of The Mall and its buildings, especially Carlton House Terrace, are under utilised and even abused.

What would you do about Carlton House Terrace?
London had a very great urban designer in John Nash, who recognised that the parklands could be enhanced by buildings. One of the great misunderstandings about buildings and parks is that people do not realize that the juxtaposition of the manmade and greenery can work brilliantly. Nash designed Carlton House Terrace; he designed the great avenue that goes up Regent Street to Regent's Park. There was a proposal in the last fifty or so years that these should all be demolished, but fortunately they were not. What makes me very angry is that the ground floor of Carlton House Terrace, which is quite wonderful, is used solely for car parking. I cannot work out who for. I do not mean the cars in front, but those inside the building. All along the ground floor, behind the pillars, are cars, presumably belonging to people who use the offices that are perhaps government

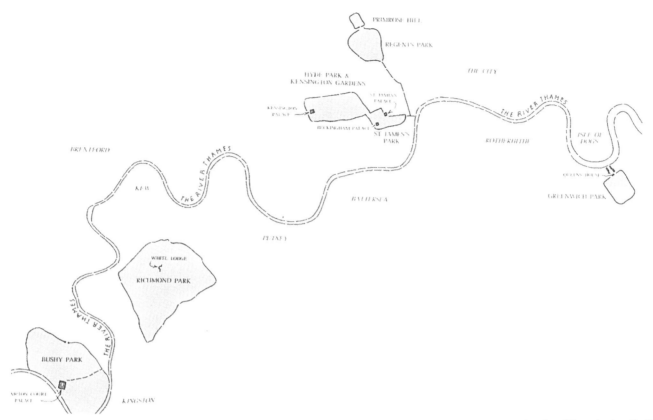

Location of the parks along the Thames

offices. And yet the only buildings for the public, like the little cafés in the trees, are like utilitarian post-war boxes. There is no joy in them. I think there should be cafés in Carlton House Terrace for all the tourists that walk down there, for the people who come to the palace and visit the parks. These buildings should be for the public. Why are they car parks? In this green age, when we are trying to limit the use of the car, this is something we should transform. Nash and others over a hundred years ago built magnificent monuments that we have filled with cars and offices. I think that is wrong.

Carlton House Terrace is a wonderful terrace with a fine plinth. You could make openings and put terraces and tables on wooden decks, as they have done at Somerset House: the café on the river there is a real treasure; it is a great place to see the river and it enhances the building itself. You could do the same here where there are many more passing pedestrians. People could enjoy the view of soldiers on parade and of the park. That is one scheme I feel very strongly about.

So it is partly anger at what is happening and partly frustration at lost opportunities that make me continuously become involved in advocating change. But not a very big physical change. Creating a café is not like building a giant motorway; it does not involve huge sums of money, only small change. The big change would be a change in attitude to our institutions. After all, this is public space and should be used for the enjoyment of London and its great institutions in a way that would enhance London's public realm.

You are making a broader point about the public realm?
What is the public realm? What were the royal routes? What was Constitution Hill where the monarch walked up and down to take his constitutional, or Rotten Row where the King would ride. These are public places now, and the parks are public. The best bit of London's public realm is these routes, the parks, and the connections. The concept of a public realm is not ill formed in London but we are not quite sure what is public, what we have and what we do not have. It has been in transition for some time and I would just like to

push that transition a bit further, a bit faster because there is the potential for us to enjoy here a public realm that is really quite sublime, one of the finest in the world. But it is a little ill thought through at the moment; the connections are not properly formed and we have not grasped the potential. My feeling is that if we pushed a bit further and examined these connections we could have a world-class public realm, really fine areas to be in, to move in, to experience. This would be true city making.

Why do we need a public realm? Why is there a need for a public realm and celebrations there?
It may sound something of a contradiction but in this world of media communications we are discovering the importance of a public realm more and more. When we look at television or a film of, say, the Great North Run crossing the wonderful bridges of the River Tyne, we realise that the Tyne bridge and the streets of Newcastle are where all those thousands of people gather. I have seen magnificent firework displays on Princes Street in Edinburgh. People are becoming more and more aware that cities can be something much more than places for working and just living. The public realm areas of British cities are being redefined. Some would say that there is an urban renaissance. And London is not only a city for the people who live in it: it is the capital city, a walled city. And our public realm here is on a larger scale. Great events have taken place in Hyde Park: the funerals of Queen Elizabeth the Queen Mother and Princess Diana; the processional routes of weddings; the celebrations on winning the World Cup and victory after the Second World War. They all happened inside the public realm. And when we walk there outside these celebrations we have a memory of those great events. And we share these public spaces as part of our shared living rooms, out in the streets, and parks, and squares. They are what unite us. They are what we have outside our private dwellings, beyond our television screens. The public realm is having quite a renaissance and here in London we have the scope to reinforce it in an extraordinary way.

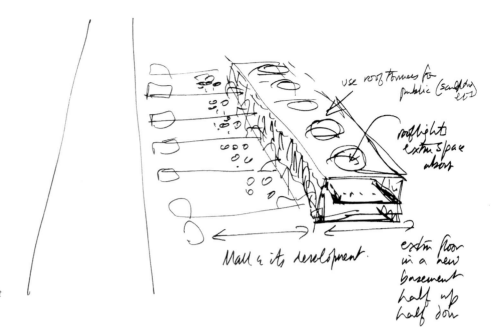

use roof tower for
public (scaffold)

rooflights
extra space
above

Mall & its development.

extra floor
in a new
basement
half up
half down

Right: Sketch by Terry Farrell of The Mall and its development
Opposite: A result of the parks proposals is that The Mall
would become a lively, pedestrian-friendly thoroughfare.
Small pavilions housing cafés would be placed under trees
along the wide carriageway on the north flank of The Mall,
which at present is used for car parking

*Is there some emotional, ethical drive behind your proposals
or are they purely pragmatic thoughts about the renaissance
of London?*

I have always had strong feelings that the way our institutions
of government and the way the monarchy relates to them are
not fully resolved and do not have the happiest relationship
with the people of Britain in terms of helping them
understand how we are governed. The accessibility of the
institution somehow creates the feeling of a nanny state:
there is somebody up there looking after us. But in reality it is
not like that. If there is a moral issue that I feel strongly about
it is not pro or against monarchy, it is that we should have a
more visible, more explicit set of institutions. And these
should be not only explicit in terms of the rules and the
accessibility of the rules, but also in how they are expressed
physically on the ground. Putting a big wall around a garden
and a blank façade says something about impenetrability. I
have a problem with that; and if there is a morality it is about
trying to readdress the relationship of our buildings and our
spaces within cities and particularly within London, and round
the royal parks, so that they better express the reality of our
time and we all benefit more from them. For me that is where
the most important issues lie.

I think a lot about the potential of London. I get angry
about the potential because other great cities have got their
act together. You go to Berlin, re-building itself now that the
wall is down, and Berlin is reinventing its public realm in the
most extraordinary way. It is relying on history; they are
looking at the way Berlin used to be, but they are building a
new Berlin. We have never got ourselves together to build
London the way it should be in today's age. I think we could
take the gardens, the parks, the palaces and be better than
any of them. Not that it is a competition, but I think we need
to learn from others. I think London is sitting on a treasure
house of palaces and parks that could make the greatest
public realm of practically any other city in the world, and so I
get angry at the lack of recognition and the stick-in-the-mud
attitude that this is a Victorian creation and so cannot be
disturbed. We are doing nothing when we could do so much
for London, not only environmentally but in order to release

some of the inhibitions about our institutions, about the
relationships of monarchy, government and people. These
places could speak volumes about these new relationships and
they could open up a public realm and a way of relating that
would be exhilarating and would make this great city that is
London much, much greater.

It is very important to understand the difference between
London and other great cities that are planned as capital cities
and that express the relationship of the institutions of
government with the public realm, because when you place
government buildings, palaces, in the streets of the city, you
have to recognise the relationship between the streets, the
public realm, and what such buildings represent. I studied
urban design in America and was fascinated by the way their
politics and constitution have a very visible organisation and
structure. When they planned Washington, that structure was
made into architecture. It is no accident that Thomas
Jefferson, one of the co-authors of the Declaration of
Independence was an architect himself. When you look at
Washington, the Capitol, the White House, and the great
monuments, they are all set in a public realm that makes
explicit how their country works. Clearly London is not like
that; there is something perverse about London: with the
screen in front of Buckingham Palace, with the new railings at
10 Downing Street, and with the Prime Minister living in a
little side street that you cannot get to now, it is almost as if it
is getting more obscure rather than clearer. I am not
proposing for a minute that we should follow the model of
Washington or Paris. They have different kinds of government. But we should examine our institutions, and how they
express themselves, and how they are set in a public realm.
We should ask if this is right for us, and we should be more
conscious of ways in which we can make them better for us
and thus give better meaning to our city. When you look at
Paris from the air it is a fantastic city but London is a great city.
In Paris the great avenues are built around an existing city,
and so in some ways it has more meaning and more relevance
to London. Washington was built from scratch but in Paris the
great monuments sit on avenues and vistas that are carved
through a mediaeval street plan, and what you see there are

avenues that are public spaces. The Mall does not seem like a public space. When you look at their malls, their great avenues, there are shops and restaurants and people living next to them whereas ours is set in this parkland where perhaps people lived in palaces once, but they are not there today. There are offices in Carlton House Terrace; the Buckingham Palace façade is really an empty husk that is not occupied; the royal family is not in there. There is something to learn from these cities about how they express themselves, how they give vitality and meaning to their cities in a way that London could also have had but does not have today.

But what gives you the right to re-design Buckingham Palace? If you were my neighbour I would move.
I believe that the space between our buildings, the public realm, is a shared part of our world. It is of great value, greater than that of the individual house in that we all want wonderful streets and wonderful squares. That is why the first thing we consider when choosing a house is where it is, not the house itself. You would not want to live in the finest house in the world in the middle of a terrible slum or a war zone. You would live in a good house or even an average house if it was set in a magnificent street, if it was located in one of the best cities in the world, in a fine place. Place begins with the outdoors and here at Buckingham Palace, it is our realm, a public realm, in which I include everyone: every citizen, every person in Britain, the royal family, the government, everybody. We should all comment and all try and see whether we can raise our game; and we should all make suggestions. I am making suggestions about the public realm as a citizen of Britain. I am not interfering with some private individual's house. I am concerned primarily with the interface between the public spaces, the interfaces between the palace and everything around it. At the moment it is very unsatisfactory because it has never adjusted to the changes in the monarchy from the time when these were not just private palaces, but private palaces and parkland. The public has taken over the parkland and the avenues and the drives of the park, and the royal family has retreated behind walls and put up screen buildings. That was a wrong move. It did not do anything for

the city around it and needs to evolve and improve. What I am suggesting is not at all radical. The alterations in 1912 and Nash's transformation in 1820 were far more radical. These proposals take more account of history and continuity in urban design terms than those changes perpetrated in previous centuries.

You want four slightly larger mouseholes but keep the front and make the walls more transparent. Could you not be more radical? Why not introduce glass, trim the tailfins a bit?
I feel strongly that an urbanist, an urban designer should stimulate society in its public realm by making suggestions for improvements that reflect it. I am not trying to change the way the British run themselves. I am saying that what we have now does not reflect what we are. I am trying to reflect what we are and where I think we are going and so I am trying to reflect the fact that every survey finds that the British people love the royal family, love continuity; and that overseas visitors see the monarchy as representing some degree of family continuity, a kind of paternity, a need for continuity that is beyond politics. Whatever my own feelings, even if I had anarchist or strong republican feelings, it would be a completely meaningless exercise for me to say that we do not need any of these institutions or that we need totally different institutions. There would be no point in proposing plans for them because nobody here would want those plans. The plans I am proposing will stimulate people to think about what we have because they are already thinking in that direction. Maybe not as fast as this, but I am showing possibilities and trying to reflect society better. After all, the great cities of Paris and Washington were reflections of what they were, not reflections of some other order. If you want a different order, if you want to live differently, then go and live somewhere else. Today you have that choice.

You are trying to reshape the palace and adjust our relationship with it but are you also thinking about democracy?
There has always been a lot of talk about democracy in this country, about it being the mother of democracy, the leader in

*Computer sequence showing the pedestrian-friendly
approach to Buckingham Palace*

democracy but in many ways our institutions are very rusty. They need oiling. Many people feel this. The Government has been looking at city government, city mayors; it has been re-thinking the House of Lords. We all know that these things evolve. During the nineteenth century and at the beginning of the twentieth century there were great changes for men and eventually for women. All those changes happened either at the time of, or just before, this building was taking shape as we know it. They were never assimilated into society. Nowadays, through the media, through electronic communi-cation, through world travel, people are thinking very hard about our institutions. Inevitably we make comparisons as we go into Europe. We are interested in the way other people do things and we should have a more flexible framework of buildings to reflect that, whilst not throwing away the best of what we have. We have some very strong institutions of government and some very, very strong buildings that reflect that.

My main critique is that the public realm around these buildings, how they interface with the public, and what they say on their public faces is not resolved. In many ways it is like a break-up sale: some people got the gardens and put a wall round them; in Greenwich, the University got a bit and the Navy and the Maritime Museum each got a bit, but they were not designed and built in bits. They were built around wonderful processional routes and gardens, and ever since we have been dividing them up and putting walls around things that do not need walls. The result of the break-up has been the creation of barriers that have seriously diminished these great set pieces.

The rediscovery that London is a great place to be and to live is part of the urban renaissance of our times and our cities. Public squares, fountains, and gathering places rather than great processional routes for cavalcades of horses are becoming an increasingly significant part of what people expect from their cities. To come to the great institutions, people want places to meet, to assemble, to have something to eat, to see an exhibition, to have public gatherings, perhaps projected on a screen as at Covent Garden where the opera being performed is projected outside in the square. And I see pavilions; I see events; I see a more deliberate programme of things happening outside the palace and inside the courtyard and in the gardens. It could be a wonderful place for concerts, like Kenwood, but occasionally, perhaps half a dozen times a year, when great statesmen visit or on great State occasions or great family occasions. We need to invent new programmes. We need to invent how society can make more use of public spaces. Manifesting the theatre of life in our public spaces is what urban design is all about. But we have put up barriers and have not fulfilled the potential. We have created disconnections. My aim is to put back meaning and opportunity into these designs.

What are the most important things that you yourself would like to resolve?

I have been involved in many urban proposals in cities, not only in Britain but overseas, and I know that there is a journey to be made. You cannot change cities without carrying the people with you and unless you become joint authors with them. But I also know that unless there is something on the table to start with, people cannot begin the conversation, because everyone has a different starting point. The important issue is to set a dialogue in motion rather than to solve everything right here and now. That is the point I am trying to make but the main issues that I would like to address immediately are the front forecourt, the buildings around it, garden screens, and possible ways through into the central courtyard of the palace.

The ethos you want is of putting ideas forward. Are you afraid of how they will be received? You are treading immensely carefully with this project.

There are those who think I am being far too bold and those who think I am not going far enough. I am not intimidated because I have nothing to gain and nothing to lose. The advantage I have is that I am doing this as a hobby and if people do not like what I do that is fine. I have put it forward more like a painter or a sculptor in my own studio than as an architect. If I paint something or make something in my studio and nobody likes it, so what? I have no official position, but it might change things. If it does not, I still found it stimulating to look at it, and I know that already there are people who respect and enjoy and share some of my thoughts. That is enough.

What are you not touching?

What am I not touching? I am not proposing to knock down the front of Buckingham Palace. I know enough about English Heritage and the force of those who want to keep things the way they are. Moreover, my own conviction is that layered history is interesting. There is no way I want to argue that Nash's building is better than the facade placed in front of it by Aston Webb, which is interesting because it reflects its time. It is like the pyramid at the Louvre: it does not destroy the buildings around it but is a total reinterpretation. The arches would be an incredible symbol; they could be in glass; they could be lit at night and be blue; or they could be in stone and very simple. But they are an opportunity to make a very physical, a very clear iconic that is a symbolic way of saying that this is change, this is different. Just as the Louvre gets connected through the pyramid, here connectedness is also the story. The arches would be the most radical thing but in people's minds the walls are an extraordinarily important symbol of the Queen and the royal family and they protect the symbolic matriarch.

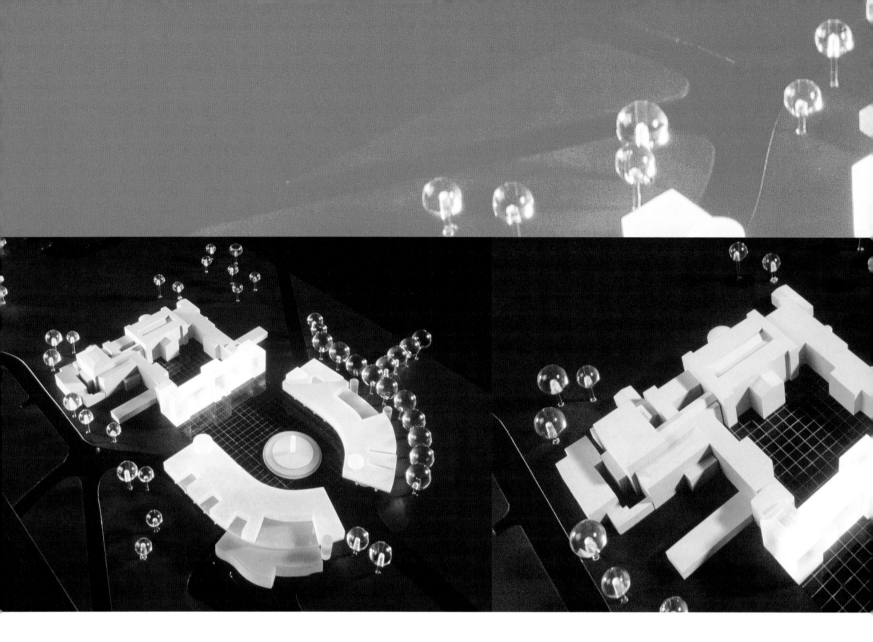

Model showing the perforated screen wall, new
public square and covered colonnade

Was there an outcry from the Establishment before the Aston Webb façade was built?
When Aston Webb was redoing the front, the British establishment, because of the strength of Victoria's reign and the success of the Empire at the beginning of the twentieth century, could do as much or as little as they liked to Buckingham Palace without fear of anyone objecting.

At that time, during the First World War, my grandfather was sent to places all around the world. He did not know where he was or what he was doing there but he knew he was there for king and country. And I think that people thought that 'those up there' knew best. They thought themselves incredibly lucky to be British and incredibly lucky to be on the winning side. If the manager of the winning team was all for it, then no questions were asked.

The front of Buckingham Place was changed without a consensus. Today, we live in different times. Those were realistic although not bad times, any more than they were good times. The Aston Webb front was a screen. It put a veil across what had happened to the monarchy. It was built at a time when there was so much power behind the British Establishment that it could get away with it as it could not have done at any other time.

As a result the screen is anti-social and it divided us. But for some this division was a good thing. They wanted the grandeur of the great leaders, or the apparent great leaders to be perceived by all. But this can be a fickle thing. If the leadership is not really taking the people where they want to go then they should question the symbols of that leadership. We need to move ahead with that both sensitively and appropriately.

Is there a privacy we need to respect?
I think the privacy issue for the royal family or whoever lives in the palace – and I believe there are many people other than the royal family that live there – is an odd one, because privacy is a suburban concept. I would expect someone to have privacy in their house in the country or in a genuinely private house, but these palaces were never private houses. The houses of great princes and monarchs were public places. They were places for visitors of state from overseas to be entertained, for the great men of the country to come to for festivities in the gardens. They were built to be enjoyed as great public places. After all they are a kind of city in themselves rather than private dwellings.

The idea that behind that wall Prince Charles is walking his dog and nobody should intrude is a modern suburban idea and is not part of the concept of palace, great grounds, great parks, or public realm as it then was. It was a place for the monarchy and for the general public.

If you are thinking about treading lightly, what are you uncertain about?

The question of whether I feel convinced or not about these ideas is a difficult one for me to answer. The way to proceed to a broad view, to a master plan, is to come up with a concept that you articulate, advocate and put forward. Then you wait for responses and when those responses come they are often surprising.

All I know at the moment is that I need to put forward with conviction something that is strong and that is basically a hypothesis to be tested.

Why not be more radical?

There are those who feel that the only way forward is to completely re-do the building or demolish it and build again. Other architects may come up with something braver. One of the things that happens often, as it did in the area around St Paul's Cathedral or the South Bank, is that I have suggested that the mould be broken and there were strong objections. Then, eventually, through persuasion, people start to think that maybe there is something in this; and then they all agree that there is something in it, and suggest something even bolder. Perhaps someone will suggest glass façades or taking it all down. I am fully open to that. Urban transformations, urban rethinking mean that we have to rethink our own

stability, the way in which we want to hang on to what is familiar, and then challenge that in steps. I think that the British in particular are in need of that.

And so in the design process for Buckingham Palace this is the thinking of an advance party?

I like the idea that this is a reconnaissance exercise. I think that is right. I do not believe in being tentative in a reconnaissance and some will think that this is sacrilege, that it is high treason. But others will say that it is wishy washy, that we should not tiptoe around it but change the institution boldly. But many of those who want bold changes actually avoid even looking at these great centres of excellence and quality; they build on the river or, thirty years ago, at Milton Keynes or wherever. I feel that the real quality is here and we should tackle it here. It may be that the right answer is much, much bolder than what I am proposing but we shall not get there without questioning very slowly, one step at a time, what it represents for us, what it means to us as British people, as Londoners. I have always found that you cannot question in the abstract. You have to put an idea on the table and say 'what if?' There are so many imaginative people around, not just architects and landscape designers but others who will come up with ideas if they feel it is possible. What I would like to be is an advance party for the possible.

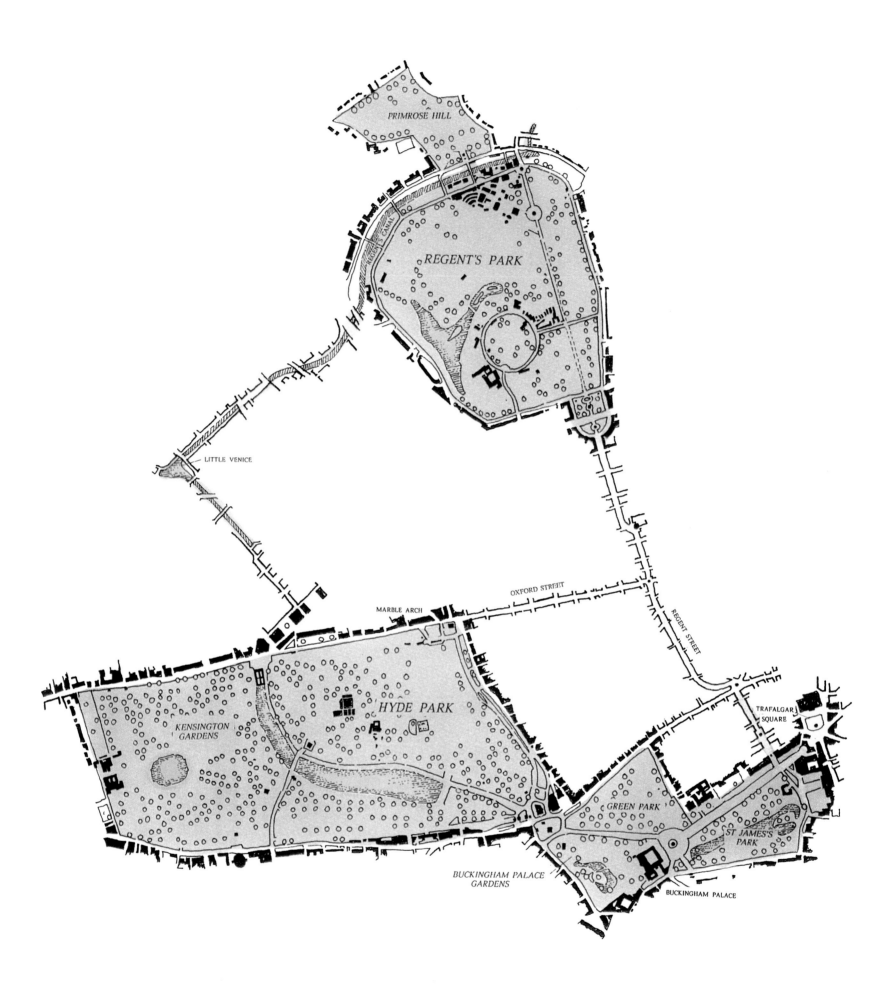

PRIMROSE HILL

REGENT'S PARK

REGENT'S CANAL

LITTLE VENICE

OXFORD STREET

MARBLE ARCH

REGENT STREET

HYDE PARK

KENSINGTON GARDENS

TRAFALGAR SQUARE

GREEN PARK

ST JAMES'S PARK

BUCKINGHAM PALACE GARDENS

BUCKINGHAM PALACE

Urban Connections

The Royal Parks and London

Since the 1990s, when he was a member of the Royal Parks Review Group, Terry Farrell has been involved with the large-scale design of the landscape of the parks and the buildings within. This has led to an on-going preoccupation with what was royal, and therefore once private, but is now in the public realm and how to make the best of this changed situation. Undoubtedly, royal privilege and heritage created places of exceptional value. That these spaces are now largely in the public domain enriches London immeasurably. But we have to ensure that what has been handed down to us is not debased or municipalised. What is the way forward today, now that we have neither an all-powerful monarchy nor the freedom to incorporate the parks fully into the public domain? It is a sad state of affairs that while royalty does not enjoy the parks as they used to, the populace cannot exploit them as fully as their designers intended.

A good example of this is the grand royal axis at Greenwich. Most people do not know that it even exists. The demise of this historic route for royal use has not led to its hand-over to the populace. We still enter via the 'tradesmen's entrance' to visit Greenwich's great buildings and spaces. Yet with the combined association of Britain's three great architects (Wren, Hawksmoor and Inigo Jones), naval history and the history of astronomy and navigation, this great but hidden axis links sites of world importance. How would the park's original designers adapt this masterpiece so that today's society could use the parks in an inspiring way?

Just as Greenwich could be grand and Versailles-like, the other parks need to regain their splendour for the benefit of modern democracy. The relationship between Kensington Palace and Kensington Gardens falls far short of the original designers' intentions: neither royalty nor the people win. The original design sequence was from the front door to the interior of the building, out to the intimate gardens and then to the landscape beyond. Owing to subsequent changes, the occupied parts have become introverted and the insignificant gardens have no relationship to the park beyond. It appears to be a less-than-happy, almost siege-like situation that results from the security that is thought to be necessary to protect the

royal family today. On the other hand, the public go through a side door to see the palace, and whilst they have full access to the park side of the garden, they have little appreciation of the original grand plan – the continuity from indoors to outdoors as one set piece.

The connection between St James's Palace and St James's Park has been lost in all but name. To come down from Piccadilly to a great and wonderful building with its axially placed clock tower, but then not to be able to progress to the park beyond is surely a sad state of affairs. The fence onto The Mall, like the wall around Buckingham Palace, indicates royalty in a state of siege: the two sides, public and royal, divide a great set piece at the most crucial point of its design. The public has no grasp of the original order. And nobody wins, especially not the architects and landscape designers who once created such wonderful places. The palace walls diminish London.

At Regent's Park, pedestrian routes from the vantage point of Primrose Hill down to the centre of London are blocked by age-old concepts of private interest that are no longer relevant. Meanwhile, the public pays for the upkeep of the central spaces. Routes through Park Square and London Zoo need to be released to the public in order to allow Nash's vision to be reinterpreted for modern times. The wonderful view from Primrose Hill and the Broad Walk should be linked directly with a pedestrian avenue through the Zoo. Further south, the Broad Walk should continue through Park Square and Park Crescent Gardens – taking very little land to do so – and thus link Regent's Park, the Underground station and Portland Place in one accessible and direct vista.

Hyde Park Corner epitomises the confused value judgements. The grand royal route up Constitution Hill, through the Wellington Arch and the Decimus Burton screen connects Green Park to Hyde Park. Although visually strong, it is hardly ever used by pedestrians and is dominated by traffic. Pedestrians – the real park users – travel underground from Green Park to Hyde Park like moles, in the most disgraceful, sensory-deprived rat runs. Yet with adjustments to the traffic lights (which are slowly being implemented), the pedestrian could walk on the surface through the great arches and screens without depriving the monarchs of their occasional use. St James's Park, Green Park, Hyde Park and Kensington Gardens should be connected in splendour for everyone. Royalty and the public would both benefit from the reinstatement of the style and splendour of the original designs for the linked landscape and buildings.

Parks and pedestrians go together. Action should be taken at Park Lane, Hyde Park Corner, Marble Arch, Regent's Park and its connections, as well as Greenwich, so that they are all fully accessible, fully enjoyable public places of world stature.

Up river, the various aspects of the study are still emerging. Hampton Court is experienced as a complete set piece but it has no royal residence. Can there not be a happy balance that gives life and accessibility? We are able to see Versailles and other uninhabited palaces as the designers intended. Unlike the French, we have a royal family, and the museum-like quality of Versailles does not need to pervade the great British palaces. They can, and should, seem alive and lived in but without barriers. The aim is to express the singularity of the original design concept and, hopefully, a united sense of purpose between the royal family and the public as joint custodians of our heritage. Power created the opportunity but the designers' vision, fantasy, skill and work actually realised these places as we see them now, and these places exist as testimony to their work and artistry.

When it comes to the future of the royal parks, we must look to the original intentions of the designers and not tinker around the edges. The parks are among the most original and sublime manmade environments in the world. At present they are neither the royal wonders of yesterday, nor the fully accessible public treasures of today. London's green trapped countryside must work better for all of us – for royalty and the people. We should work together to remain faithful to the original, inspired designs, even though society and the political order have evolved and changed.

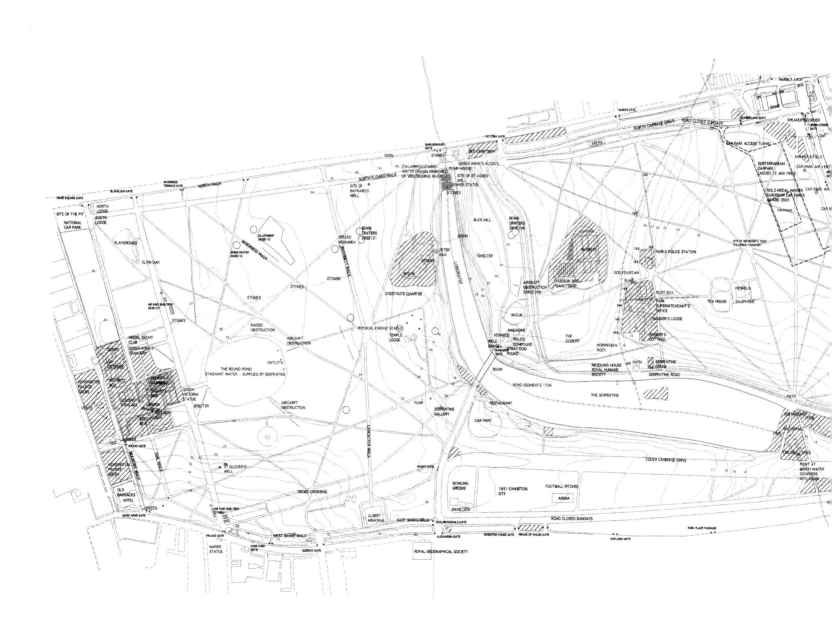

Main: Plan of Hyde Park and St James's Park showing
the various layers of activity, from access points and
subways, to an underground carpark, and areas of
restricted public access (hatched).
Below: Evolution of water bodies in St James's Park
From left to right: c..1400, 1660, 1800, 1923

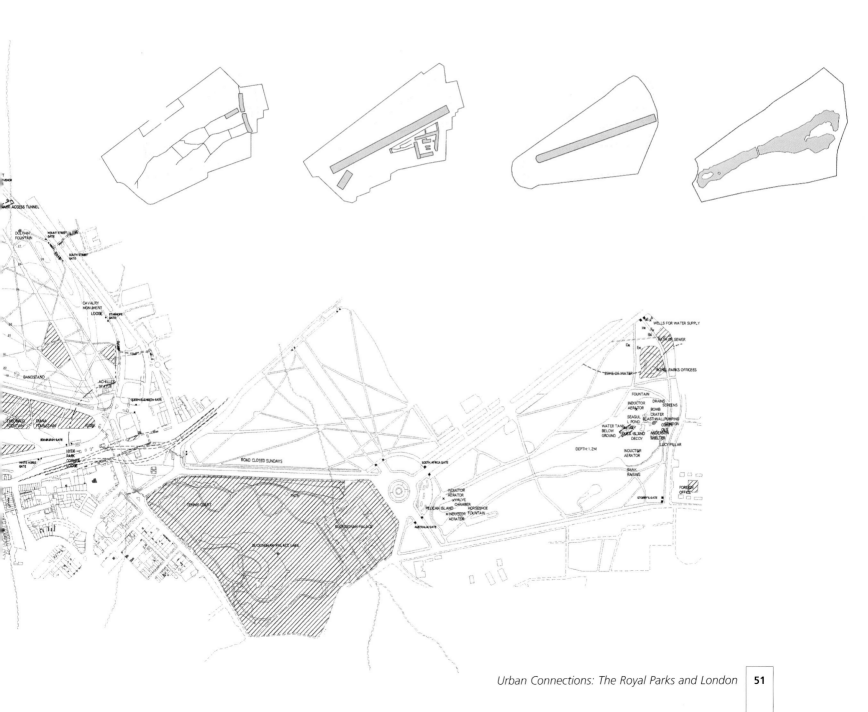

*Left: Photographs taken for Terry Farrell's
Royal Parks Review, which put forward the
case for pedestrians over cars
Opposite: Plan of Park Lane showing the street-level
crossings on the northbound carriageway*

Pedestrians coming out of Hyde Park encounter the absolutely appalling underpass system at Hyde Park Corner where they have gradually been reduced to tunnelling moles rather than those who should be most privileged to enjoy the parklands. The whole length of Park Lane's northbound carriageway was once part of Hyde Park and the 'improvements' made to the roundabouts at either end were effected to increase the speed of traffic and force pedestrians to cross solely by underpasses. But pedestrians and underpasses do not go together: as soon as one is introduced into London, the area becomes a pedestrian no-go area. It is only when Park Lane and its two roundabouts, one at each end, were introduced, that a suburban motorway system was brought into the centre of the usually pedestrian-friendly West End.

A connection from Green Park to Hyde Park, through Constitution Arch and the Decimus Burton screen would overcome the ensuing traffic congestion and would place the pedestrian walking the royal route from park to park in a privileged position.

All the underpasses would be closed and the land occupied by roundabouts would become part of the parks. It is vital that pedestrians be given paramount importance and direct surface access to the parks. What is astonishing is that all this could be achieved with almost no new engineering, the sole investment being the landscaped pedestrian surfaces, new sets of traffic lights and reprogramming of the existing lights.

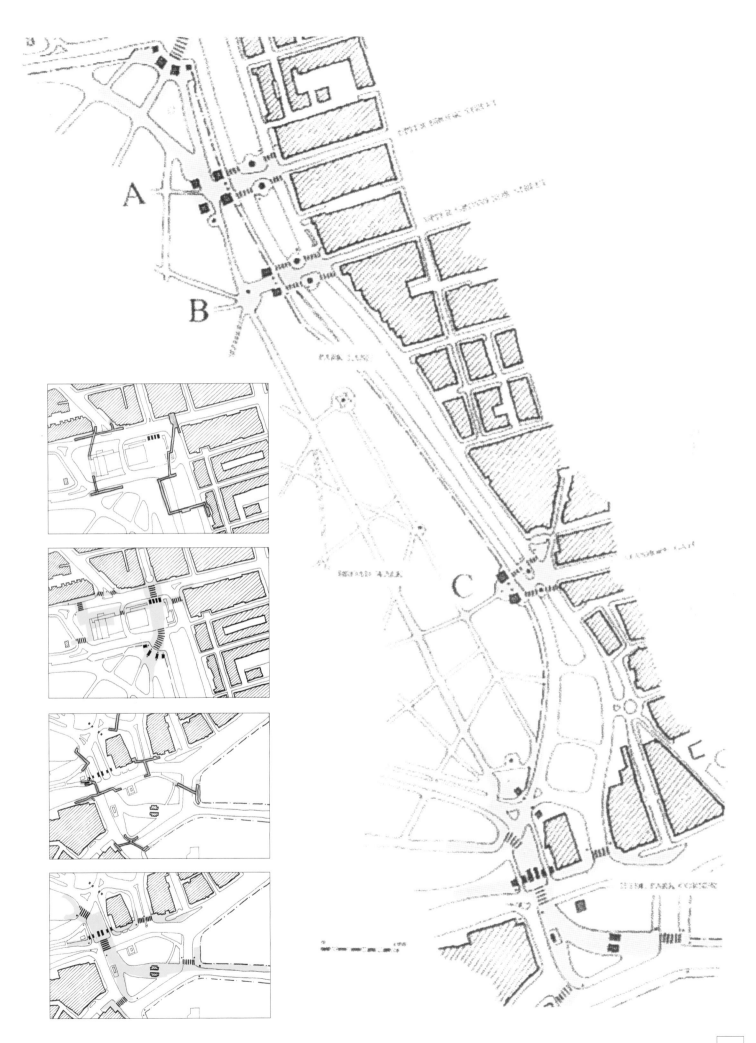

World Squares

Trafalgar Square and its surroundings

Terry Farrell & Partners' World Square proposals included an analysis of Trafalgar Square, which forms part of the ceremonial route from Buckingham Palace to St Paul's and the City

London has played centre stage among the world's great cities and has boasted, for centuries, a public realm of quality and splendour that matched its place as a leading centre of culture, commerce and urban life. Throughout Europe and Britain, decline in the public domain is being challenged with a determination to revitalise the urban fabric and create town and city centres where the quality of life and civic pride are given pride of place.

London now has its chance to have the best: to raise its profile and demonstrate that it values its citizens and its visitors, and the part they play in maintaining a vigorous centre for a world-class city. Terry Farrell & Partners' World Squares proposal examined Trafalgar Square and its surroundings as being the symbolic and physical heart of both London and the nation in general.

Trafalgar Square sits within a great amphitheatre of space – the National Gallery is its backdrop and St Martin's in the Fields, Canada House and South Africa House are its wings. Yet it has also functioned as a traffic roundabout.

Like the proposals for Buckingham Palace and the royal parks, the masterplan for Trafalgar Square looks at placing the emphasis on the movement of people rather than on traffic as well as creating a series of connected and legible landscaped routes and places.

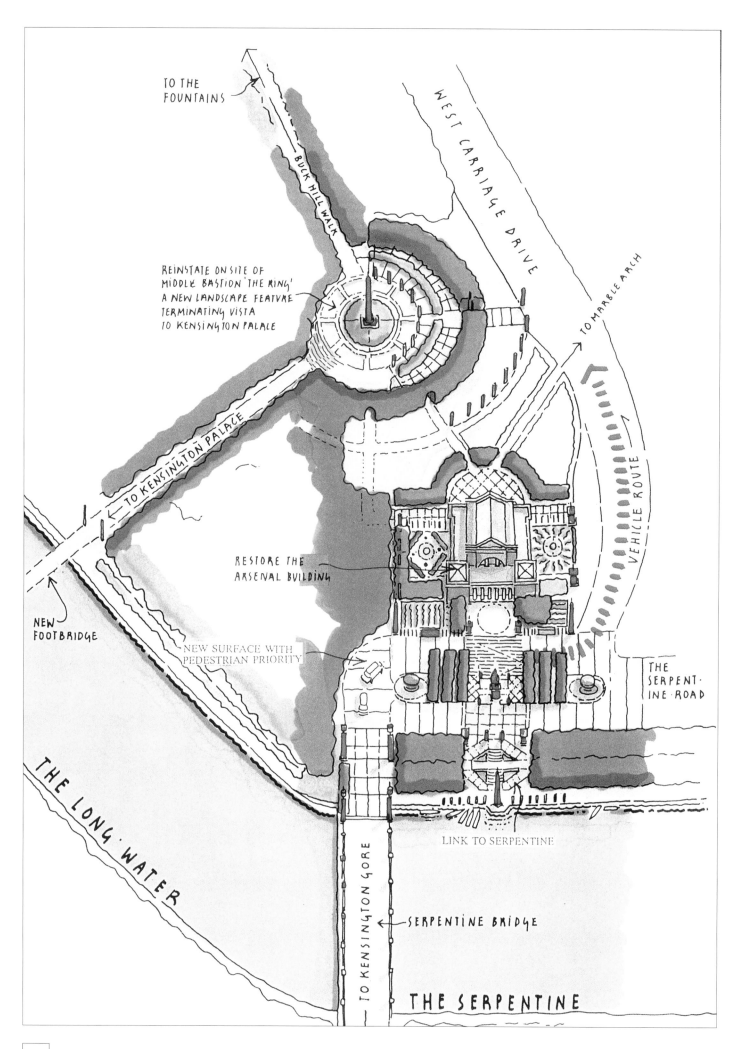

TO THE
FOUNTAINS

WEST CARRIAGE DRIVE

BUCK HILL WALK

REINSTATE ON SITE OF
MIDDLE BASTION 'THE RING'
A NEW LANDSCAPE FEATURE
TERMINATING VISTA
TO KENSINGTON PALACE

TO MARBLE ARCH

TO KENSINGTON PALACE

VEHICLE ROUTE

RESTORE THE
ARSENAL BUILDING

NEW
FOOTBRIDGE

NEW SURFACE WITH
PEDESTRIAN PRIORITY

THE
SERPENT-
INE ROAD

THE LONG WATER

LINK TO SERPENTINE

TO KENSINGTON GORE

SERPENTINE BRIDGE

THE SERPENTINE

Hyde Park

Below: Hyde Park, evolution of footpaths, 1200-2000
Bottom: Alternative proposals for North Carriage Drive:
left: existing North Carriage Drive; centre: no driveway,
landscape continues in its place; right: keep hard
landscaping for dedicated special events
Opposite: The Arsenal Building as proposed

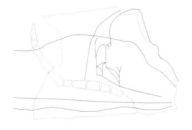 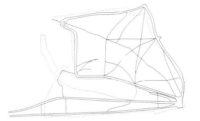 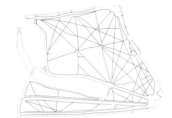 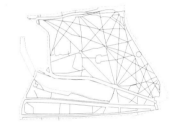

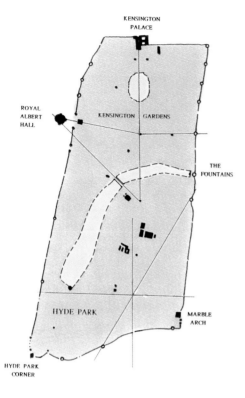

Left: Links from Kensington Gardens and
Hyde Park to the urban townscape beyond
Below: Restoration of links between
Kensington Gardens and Hyde Park
Key:
1. Hawksmoor's Orangery
2. Kensington Palace
3. New topiary gardens extending into the park
4. New sunken garden
5. New landscaped paths onto the Broad Walk
6. New direct link to the Round Pond
7. New gates
Opposite: Reinstating links from
Kensington Palace to Hyde Park

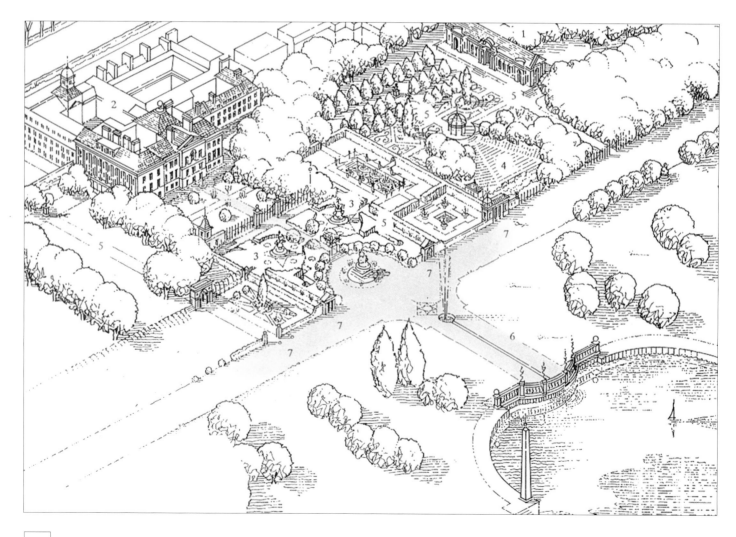

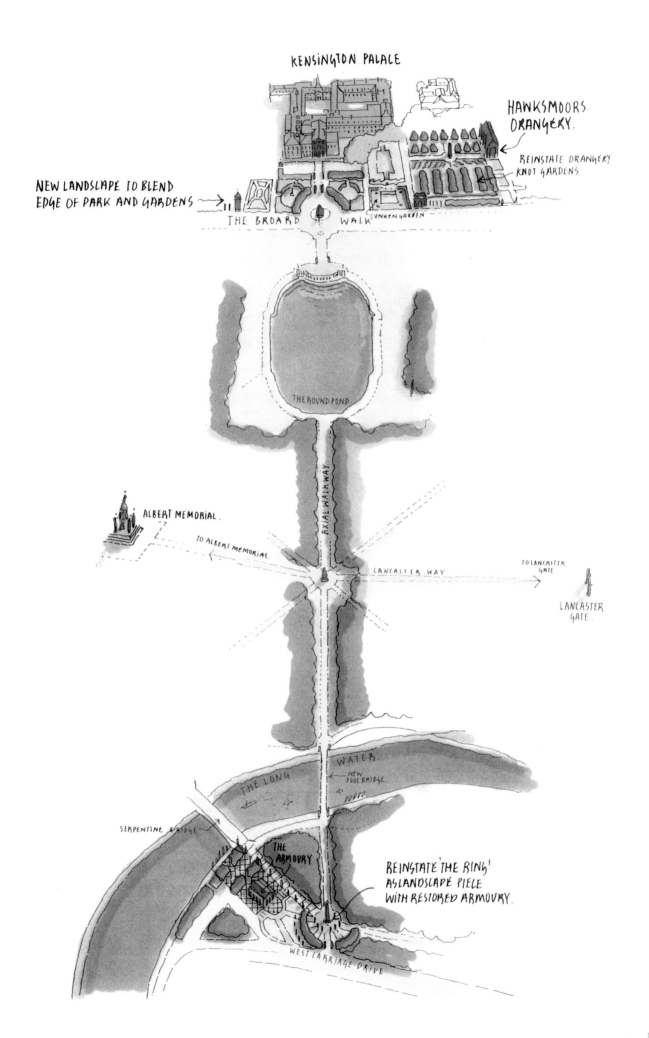

KENSINGTON PALACE

HAWKSMOORS ORANGERY.

REINSTATE ORANGERY KNOT GARDENS

NEW LANDSCAPE TO BLEND EDGE OF PARK AND GARDENS →

THE BROAD WALK

SUNKEN GARDEN

THE ROUND POND

AXIAL WALK WAY

ALBERT MEMORIAL.

TO ALBERT MEMORIAL. ←

LANCASTER WAY

TO LANCASTER GATE →

LANCASTER GATE.

THE LONG WATER.

NEW FOOT BRIDGE.

PONTO

SERPENTINE BRIDGE

THE ARMOURY

REINSTATE 'THE RING' AS LANDSCAPE PIECE WITH RESTORED ARMOURY.

WEST CARRIAGE DRIVE

Above: In spite of public opinion, the royal family has the potential to be a positive force for good. The Diana Fountain proposal sought to reinforce this view by contributing to London's public realm
Below: Views of the Serpentine

Opposite: Charles Jencks's sketch for the Diana Fountain proposal. The project was a collaboration between Jencks, who brought iconography and landscape design to the project, and Terry Farrell & Partners, who contributed to the scheme landscape and urban narrative with place making experience

The Diana Fountain

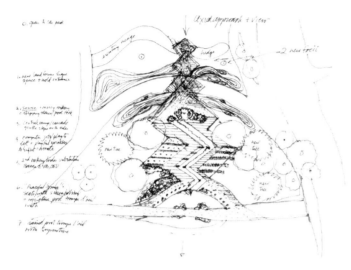

Terry Farrell & Partners' design approach for the Diana Fountain reinforces the royal family's role as a positive force for good. The submission focuses on first creating a 'place' – part landscape, part vistas and views, part focused activities – but within and connecting broadly to Hyde Park and London.

The place firstly expresses the loss, emptiness and sadness of Diana's early death. It encompasses an area of quiet contemplation, isolated seating, and still water. Secondly, like Albertopolis, the place is an act of positive commemoration, attracting and rewarding future generations of visiting children. It conserves and explains nature and wildlife. It reinforces messages of world peace and emphasises the impact that one good person can have on the world.

The place is not overly focused as to do so would destroy the character of a place that Diana came to respect. Instead, several sub-places are created, diverting and spreading visitors so that over-intensive use does not destroy the key areas of quiet and solitude.

Raised mounds on the south side protect the site from intruding traffic, give views from the Serpentine towards the Magazine and beyond and enclose play areas, pools and fountains. Densely planted areas contain natural habitats where ecology is preserved and explained. Water springs from here: it is a place of birth, optimism and early childhood.

The northern edge of the site, adjacent to the Serpentine is a shaded place of solitude that evokes stillness, quiet and contemplation. A long, still pond creates a causeway and isolation; an empty stone seat signifies loss. There is water running down the slope from the mounds above that fills the ribbon pond.

The area north of the Serpentine represents Diana's public life through a visible inclined bank leading to views of London. The Magazine becomes a place of peace, exhibiting the results of man's inhumanity and ways to turn our manufacturing ingenuity away from manufacturing war missiles.

Finally, on the upper and lower levels of this north bank, a short walk takes the visitor to the great vista back to Kensington Palace. The royal parks were once full of connected vistas. Their enhancement and restoration would greatly improve London.

Qualities of connectivity, reaching out and seeing beyond duty to responsibility and compassion provide the opportunity for improving and enhancing life – all characteristics associated with Princess Diana.

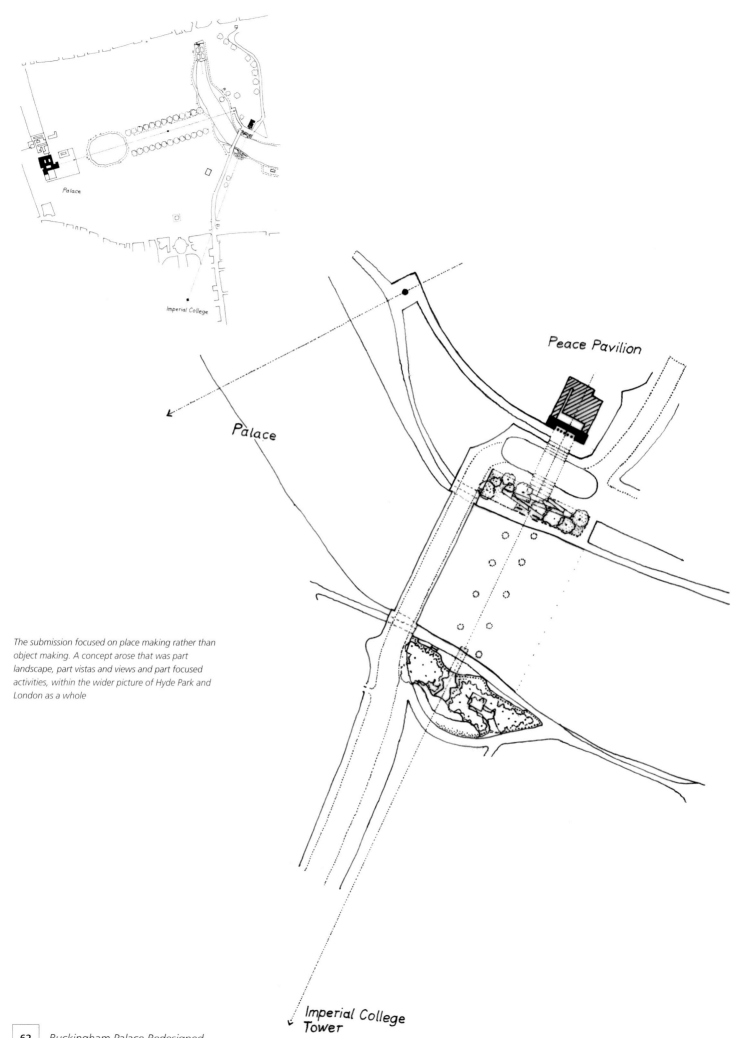

Peace Pavilion

Palace

The submission focused on place making rather than object making. A concept arose that was part landscape, part vistas and views and part focused activities, within the wider picture of Hyde Park and London as a whole

Palace

Imperial College

Imperial College Tower

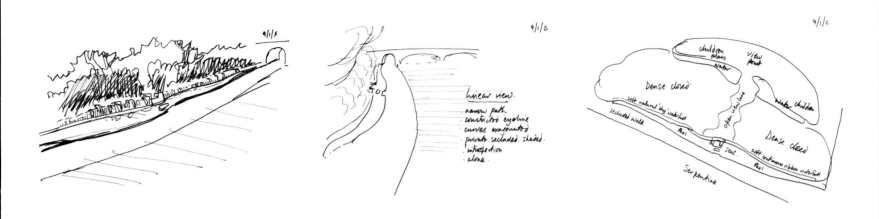

Above: Sketches by Terry Farrell
Below: The northern edge of the site adjacent to the Serpentine pathway is a place of stillness and contemplation, marked by a long, still pond and a stone seat

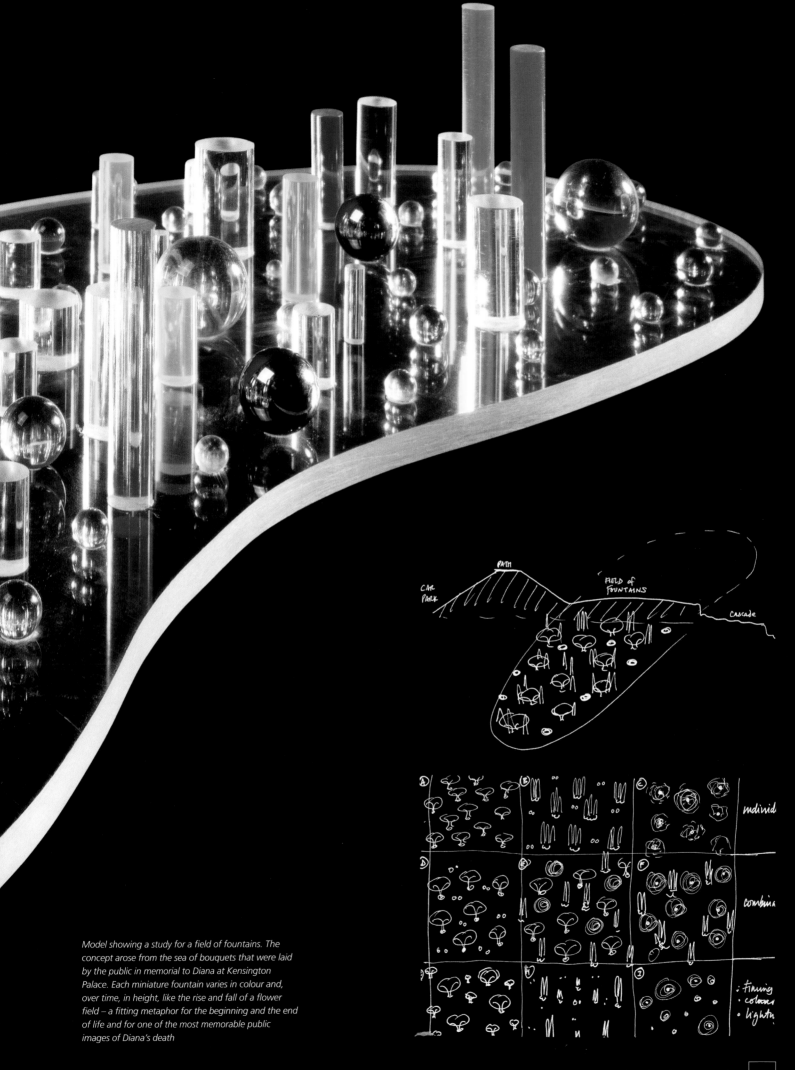

Model showing a study for a field of fountains. The concept arose from the sea of bouquets that were laid by the public in memorial to Diana at Kensington Palace. Each miniature fountain varies in colour and, over time, in height, like the rise and fall of a flower field – a fitting metaphor for the beginning and the end of life and for one of the most memorable public images of Diana's death

Above: Route through Primrose Hill and Regent's Park
to the Zoological Gardens and on to Park Crescent
Below left: Proposed route through Primrose Hill
to the Zoological Gardens
Below right: Proposed route through Park Crescent
Opposite: Plan of the pedestrian connections between
Primrose Hill, Regent's Park and on to Regent Street.

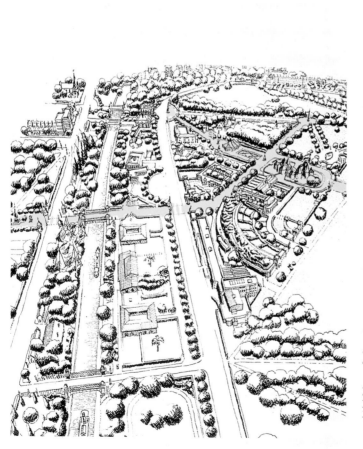

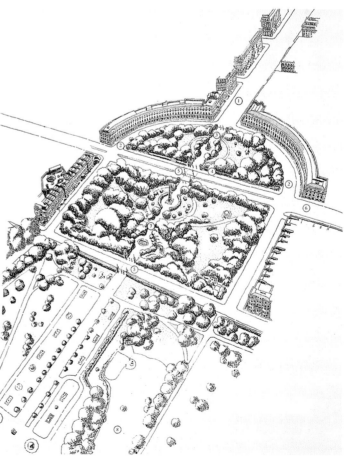

Regent's Park & Primrose Hill

Links to an Urban Townscape

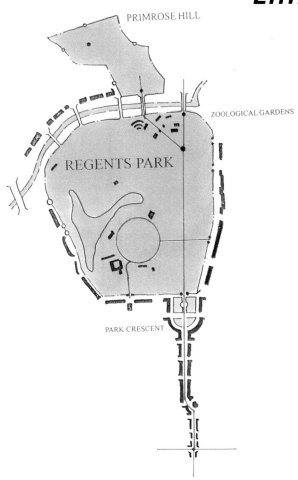

From the top of Primrose Hill to the south there is a wonderful panorama where the city's green spaces seem to connect and roll down into central London. London Zoo is the only barrier to the view – a physical intrusion into the landscape caused by the buildings themselves, the semi-privatisation of the fenced-in land and the lack of pedestrian permeability.

The proposals seek to connect the main internal routes within the zoo and make them public, so that it is possible to travel from Regent's Park to Primrose Hill via a variety of fine routes. A much better park experience would arise if the zoo and its planning were rethought and it became part of the public pedestrian infrastructure rather than being an internal island of semi-private activity.

Another major blockage is at the south end of Regent's Park, where Nash's great route from Portland Place to the Broad Walk and up through Regent's Park is interrupted by the islands of Park Square and Park Crescent where only key holders have access. It is possible to retain private areas for key holders but placed these on either side of a grand pedestrian avenue linking Portland Place directly in a straight line with the Broad Walk, with pedestrian crossings on the Euston Road and the Outer Circle. This would have the additional advantage of giving Regent's Park Underground station a

direct physical and visual connection with Regent's Park and Portland Place – it is very difficult for pedestrians to get their bearings when they arrive at Regent's Park Underground station as it has no apparent connection with the park.

These proposals would restore Nash's grand vision and complete the route from Primrose Hill to St James's Park, connecting the very centre of historic London to the Primrose Hill vantage point.

The other route that should connect from Regent's Park and Primrose Hill is the one going west along the Grand Union Canal to Paddington Basin and on to Hyde Park. It should be stressed that the Grand Union Canal should be seen as an extension of the park. It was certainly planned as such by Nash but much of this route has since been badly treated. The Lisson Grove section is very poorly managed and landscaped and its access is extremely poor. It is not possible to continue along the towpath at Blomfield Road as it is now restricted to private moorings and only key holders may exit from the gate at the end. This section could be opened up to the public, and a generous pedestrian crossing provided across Edgware Road to by-pass the tunnel. Then it would take only take a few pedestrianised streets to reconnect to the canal towpath and thence into Regent's Park.

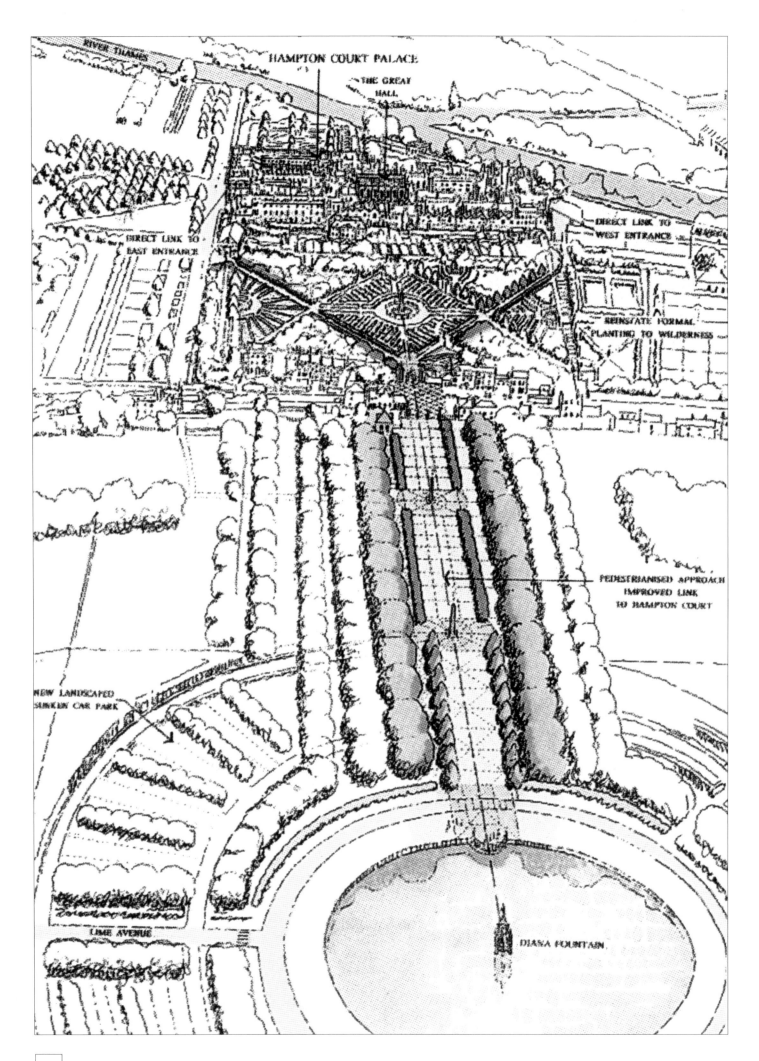

RIVER THAMES

HAMPTON COURT PALACE

THE GREAT HALL

DIRECT LINK TO
WEST ENTRANCE

DIRECT LINK TO
EAST ENTRANCE

REINSTATE FORMAL
PLANTING TO WILDERNESS

PEDESTRIANISED APPROACH
IMPROVED LINK
TO HAMPTON COURT

NEW LANDSCAPED
SUNKEN CAR PARK

LIME AVENUE

DIANA FOUNTAIN

Hampton Court

and Bushy Park

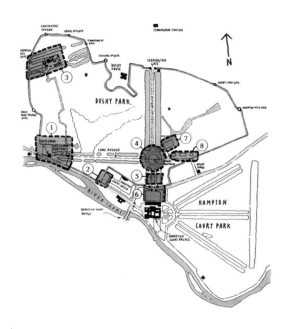

Above: Diagram indicating Bushy Park's problem areas
Key:
1. White Lodge/Lime Avenue
2. Barrack Gate car park
3. Upper Lodge
4. Diana Fountain
5. Chestnut Avenue
6. Hampton Court Gate/Lion Gate
7. Existing car park
8. Lime Avenue
Right: Proposal to reinstate new pedestrian links to Hampton Court
Key:
1. New formal landscape feature to provide improved setting for Diana Fountain
2. New landscaped and sunken car park for Bushy Park
3. New landscaped and sunken car park for Hampton Court Palace
4. New pedestrian approach to Hampton Court Gate
5. New surface finish across road to demarcate priority of vista link from
Bushy to the Wilderness and Hampton Court Palace
Opposite: View of the proposed improved link with Hampton Court

Hampton Court and Bushy Park, to the west of London, form the largest of the Royal Parks. Bushy's Chestnut Avenue vista is dominated by the silhouette of the Great Hall, which powerfully links Hampton Court Palace to the landscape of Bushy Park. This grand vista is now a dull car route.

Christopher Wren's unbuilt 'grand layout' block plan of 1689 shows the concept of a main north–south axial route through Bushy Park, while a sequence of diminishing court-yards led directly up to Henry VIII's Great Hall. Other historic plans indicate formal avenues, now mostly lost. The best example is the sadly underplayed drama of Wren's east–west Lime Avenue vista. Terry Farrell & Partners have identified several ways to reinstate the park's once-intended grandeur, including improvements to the landscape settings of public car and coach parks; reinstating lost vistas; inserting new planting around the existing Diana Fountain; pedestrianising Wren's grand vista to Hampton Court; linking Park Gate and Lion Gate with a new road surface to emphasise the vista of Chestnut Avenue; and replanting the Wilderness to reinforce direct routes to the east and west entrances to Hampton Court Palace.

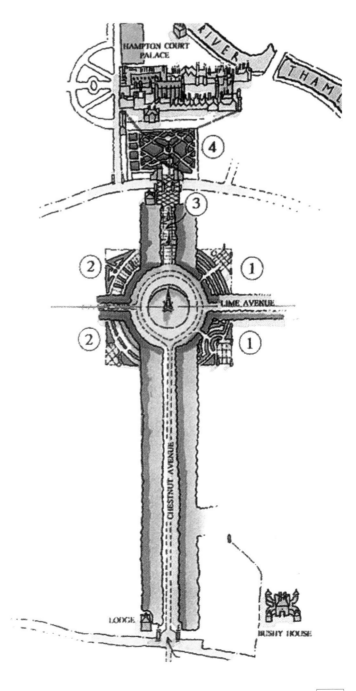

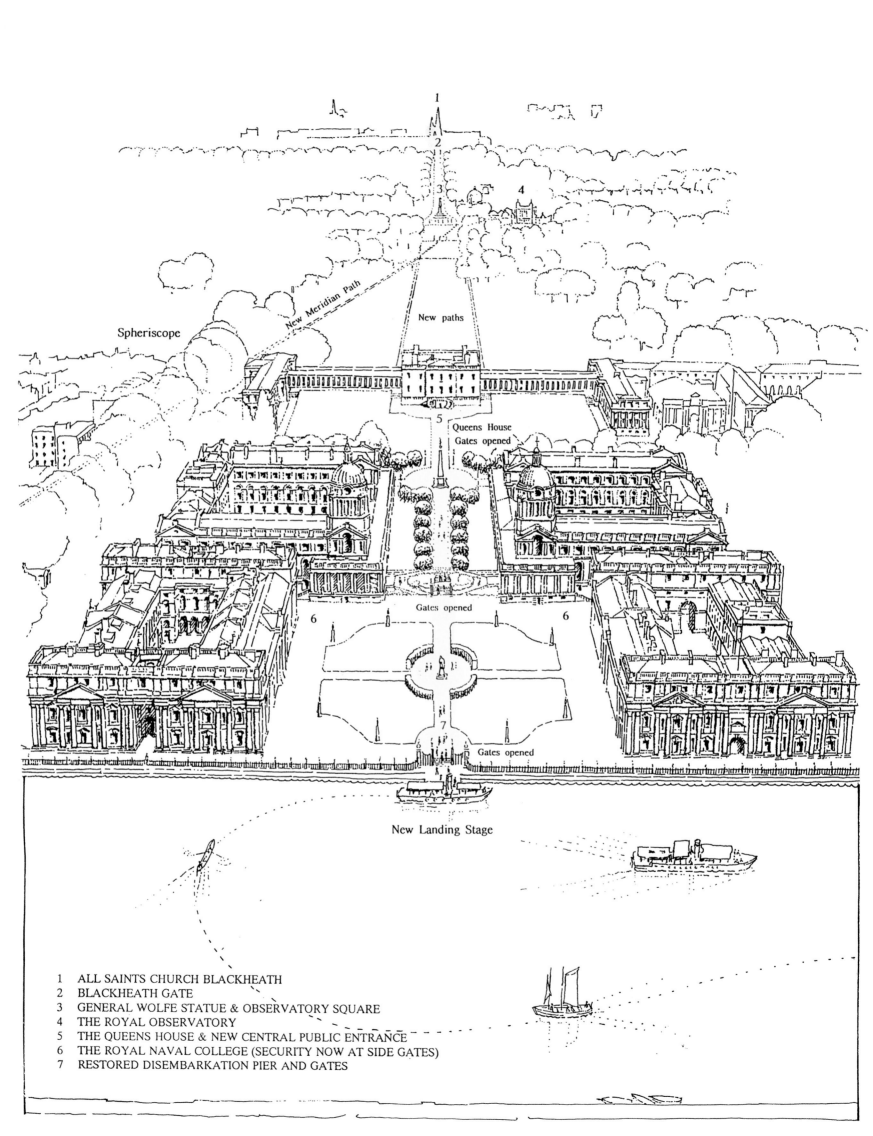

Spheriscope

New Meridian Path

New paths

Queens House
Gates opened

Gates opened

6   6

7

Gates opened

New Landing Stage

1   ALL SAINTS CHURCH BLACKHEATH
2   BLACKHEATH GATE
3   GENERAL WOLFE STATUE & OBSERVATORY SQUARE
4   THE ROYAL OBSERVATORY
5   THE QUEENS HOUSE & NEW CENTRAL PUBLIC ENTRANCE
6   THE ROYAL NAVAL COLLEGE (SECURITY NOW AT SIDE GATES)
7   RESTORED DISEMBARKATION PIER AND GATES

Greenwich
A Palace and its Park

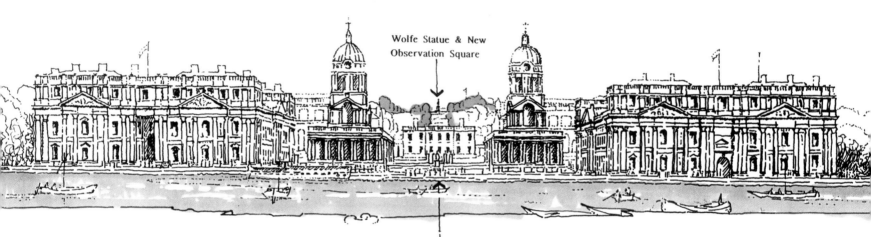

Wolfe Statue & New Observation Square

New restored Disembarkation Pier, Landing Stage and gates on Axial Vista.

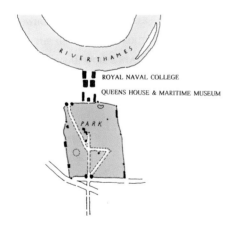

RIVER THAMES

ROYAL NAVAL COLLEGE

QUEENS HOUSE & MARITIME MUSEUM

PARK

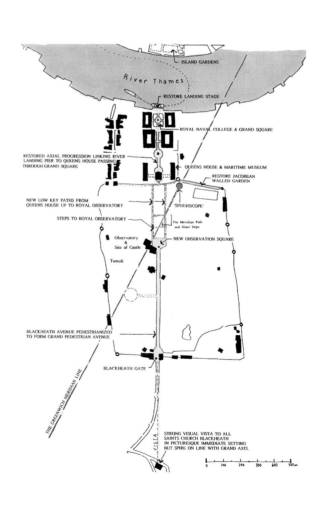

ISLAND GARDENS

River Thames

RESTORE LANDING STAGE

ROYAL NAVAL COLLEGE & GRAND SQUARE

RESTORED AXIAL PROGRESSION LINKING RIVER LANDING PIER TO QUEENS HOUSE PASSING THROUGH GRAND SQUARE

QUEENS HOUSE & MARITIME MUSEUM

RESTORE JACOBEAN WALLED GARDEN

NEW LOW KEY PATHS FROM QUEENS HOUSE UP TO ROYAL OBSERVATORY

'SPHERISCOPE'

The Meridian Path and Giant Steps

STEPS TO ROYAL OBSERVATORY

Observatory & Site of Castle

NEW OBSERVATION SQUARE

Tumuli

BLACKHEATH AVENUE PEDESTRIANIZED TO FORM GRAND PEDESTRIAN AVENUE

BLACKHEATH GATE

THE GREENWICH MERIDIAN LINE

VISTA

STRONG VISUAL VISTA TO ALL SAINTS CHURCH BLACKHEATH IN PICTURESQUE IMMEDIATE SETTING BUT SPIRE ON LINE WITH GRAND AXIS.

Top: Axial progression viewed from the river Thames
Above and right: Proposed axis re-linking the grand architectural composition of river, palace and park
Opposite: Proposed axial progression

The main concern at Greenwich is the demise of the Grand Royal Axis – both for royalty and the populace. It is proposed to reinstate the axial progression in order to link the grand architectural composition of the Queen's House and park with the River Thames. A restored river landing stage would be the starting point, or 'front door', leading to the unfolding of a sequence of great public spaces with the Royal Naval College, Queen's House and Royal Observatory as landmarks.

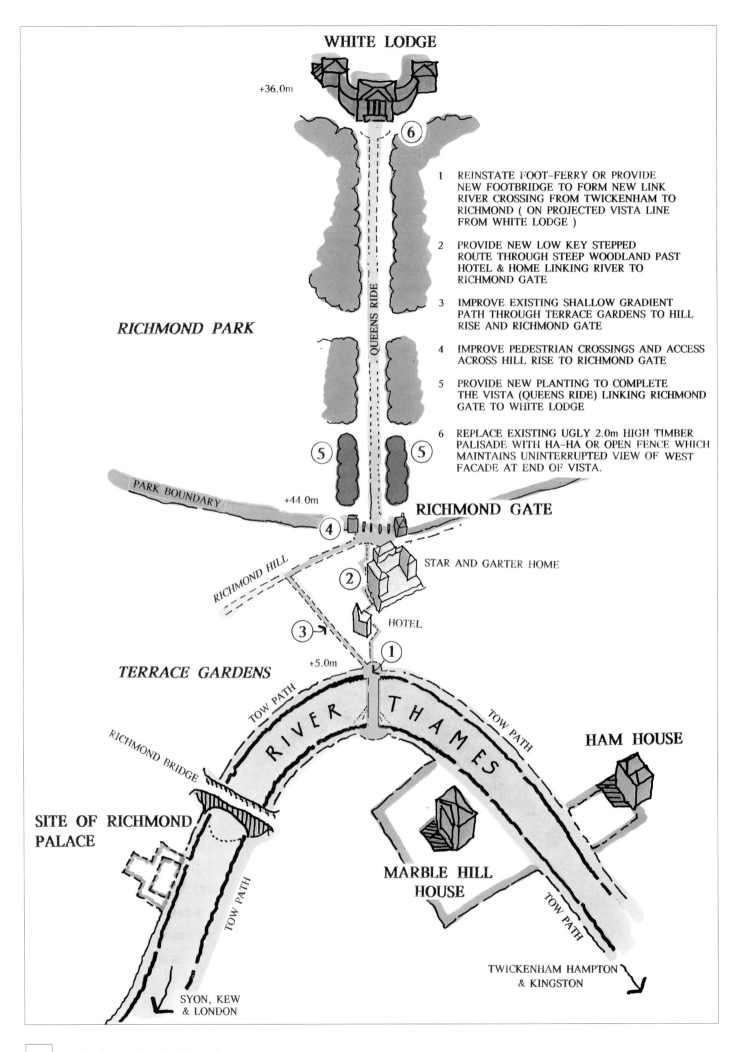

WHITE LODGE

+36.0m

⑥

RICHMOND PARK

QUEENS RIDE

1 REINSTATE FOOT-FERRY OR PROVIDE NEW FOOTBRIDGE TO FORM NEW LINK RIVER CROSSING FROM TWICKENHAM TO RICHMOND (ON PROJECTED VISTA LINE FROM WHITE LODGE)

2 PROVIDE NEW LOW KEY STEPPED ROUTE THROUGH STEEP WOODLAND PAST HOTEL & HOME LINKING RIVER TO RICHMOND GATE

3 IMPROVE EXISTING SHALLOW GRADIENT PATH THROUGH TERRACE GARDENS TO HILL RISE AND RICHMOND GATE

4 IMPROVE PEDESTRIAN CROSSINGS AND ACCESS ACROSS HILL RISE TO RICHMOND GATE

5 PROVIDE NEW PLANTING TO COMPLETE THE VISTA (QUEENS RIDE) LINKING RICHMOND GATE TO WHITE LODGE

6 REPLACE EXISTING UGLY 2.0m HIGH TIMBER PALISADE WITH HA-HA OR OPEN FENCE WHICH MAINTAINS UNINTERRUPTED VIEW OF WEST FACADE AT END OF VISTA.

PARK BOUNDARY

+44.0m

⑤   ⑤

④   RICHMOND GATE

RICHMOND HILL

②   STAR AND GARTER HOME

HOTEL

③

TERRACE GARDENS

+5.0m

①

TOW PATH   TOW PATH

RICHMOND BRIDGE

RIVER THAMES

HAM HOUSE

SITE OF RICHMOND PALACE

MARBLE HILL HOUSE

TOW PATH

SYON, KEW & LONDON

TWICKENHAM HAMPTON & KINGSTON

TOW PATH

Richmond

River and Landscape

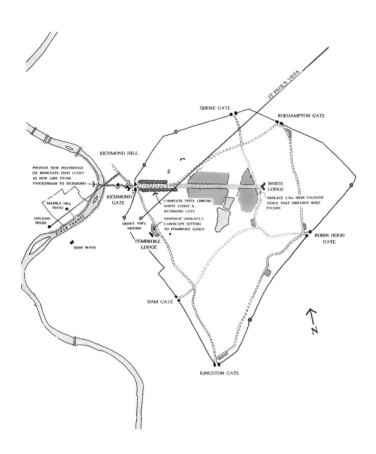

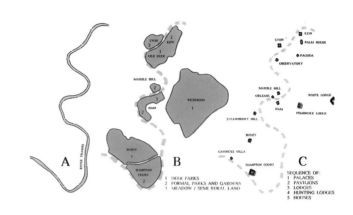

Above: Axial progression viewed from the Thames
Right: Proposed axis re-linking the grand architectural composition of river, palace and park
Opposite: Proposed axial progression

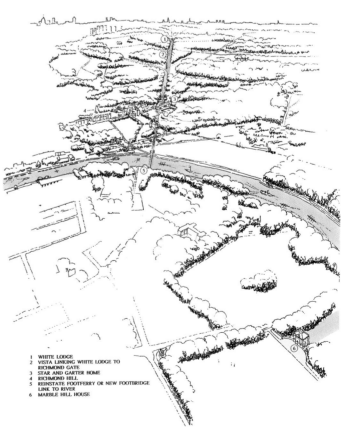

1 WHITE LODGE
2 VISTA LINKING WHITE LODGE TO
  RICHMOND GATE
3 STAR AND GARTER HOME
4 RICHMOND HILL
5 REINSTATE FOOTFERRY OR NEW FOOTBRIDGE
  LINK TO RIVER
6 MARBLE HILL HOUSE

The proposals at Richmond Park focused on reviving the vistas and grand routes between the river and parkland. Where the central London parks feature palaces in a trapped landscape, the non-urban parks (Bushy, Hampton Court and Richmond) fit within both landscape and built-up areas. Links and views to the Thames are vital. Improvement to river connections and the enhancement of the landscape to White Lodge and Pembroke Lodge are the key elements of the proposals for Richmond Park. For example, the impact of White Lodge as an architectural composition at the end of the Queen's Ride vista is reduced by the partial obscuring of the west façade by an unsightly timber fence. The land-scape to Pembroke Lodge is spoilt by parked cars. A new car park with low-ered ground level should be instated, together with a grass and gravel garden court that would link the park to the lodge and gardens.

I N T E R

What do you think of the architecture of Buckingham Palace?

I think the architecture of Buckingham Palace is rather impressive and appropriate for its purpose. It has, of course, evolved over the years. It started out as a small private house, a dower house, that was bought by George III for Queen Charlotte. It once belonged to the Dukes of Buckingham, hence the name. Its function has changed but the official court remained at St James's, which is why today ambassadors are appointed to the Court of St James's. It has since been added to. The Prince Regent's great town planning scheme started in Regent's Park and went straight down through London, culminating in the palace; and then there was the visionary scheme of George IV. Queen Victoria added a ballroom but she still regarded it as a rather small house. The present, classical front was added by Blomfield and Blore in 1913. This provided the famous balcony. In a way it was a case of architecture anticipating developments because it had not been the custom for the King and Queen or the royal family to appear in front of the palace. The first time they appeared was in 1914 when the ultimatum to Germany expired and people gravitated towards the palace. The appearance of the King and Queen thus fulfilled that very important function of displaying the monarchy to the people as the head of society. The palace has changed over the years and it has evolved from a residence to a great symbol of state. Today it is an office where the Queen conducts her business rather than her home.

Pageantry preserves our history

You have used the words 'pageantry' and 'imagination' to describe the essence of what makes a palace. What do you mean?

Our institutions are either 'dignified' or 'efficient'. The dignified institutions – the monarchy and the House of Lords – are those that appeal to the imagination, and they do appeal to the imagination. As a people we care about showing that we are a great, united nation, and the symbol of the unity of the nation is not the Prime Minister but the monarchy: the Queen and her successors.

What are the architectural aspects that help support that show?

It is the simplicity really. The classical façade is absolutely appropriate for its purpose. It is impressive, but not showy. It is not triumphalist, and right in the centre is the balcony that has become so familiar to people not only in this country but throughout the world. It had a particular significance when we were at the centre of a great empire, and it still has great significance now that we are the centre of a commonwealth. It is also the culmination of that great drive up The Mall which is used for State occasions, and that is very important. Then there is the Trooping the Colour, which is one of the great ceremonies of the year. The other one is the State Opening of Parliament, when the Queen drives in the state coach from Buckingham Palace to the Palace of Westminster and then drives back again. It is a very moving occasion. I remember a former Speaker, Lord Weatherall saying to me that when he had the job of attending on the Queen when she came back from the State Opening and was standing in the courtyard he found it so moving that tears streamed down his face. So it is a very important setting and one that works.

LORD ST JOHN
OF FAWSLEY

V I E W S

Does the word 'procession' still have a resonance and a meaning?

Absolutely. People want to see processions; they want to see the pomp of State. It is not for the glorification of the Queen; it is for assurance to other nations that we are one nation and that we are still a great nation. And one of the things that makes us a great nation is our history. Pageantry preserves our history. That is why I look with dismay at those who seek to strip our public life of pageantry because what they are really doing is separating us from our history and if we are separated from our history we are cut off from our roots and become of much less consequence.

What do you like about Buckingham Palace?

I like the gardens very much but, like all great facilities, if you overrun them they are destroyed, and this is one of the great problems of our time. I also like the interior of the palace, which is now open to the public in the summer. This is a very important development that has proved a major attraction both to ourselves and to foreign visitors.

One of the great experiences of walking through those drawing rooms is that you get a sense of history and a chance to see some of the most marvellous pictures in the world. There is another way in which the palace has developed and that is in the Queen's Gallery. This is to the left of the palace on what was the site of the Royal Chapel, the one building that was destroyed in the Second World War and not rebuilt. This has become the Queen's Gallery where there are regular exhibitions throughout the year enabling people to see different parts of the Queen's collection. It is one of the most interesting galleries in London and one of the least appreciated. John Simpson, a classical architect has just redesigned it for the Queen's Golden Jubilee.

Buckingham Palace is not like Versailles; it has a domestic character about it, dating back to its origins

Have you seen that huge piece of marble in the garden?

Yes, it is all right, but I am not mad about it. It is so monumental. It is too big, I think, for a garden that is really an English garden, which is something intimate and on a small scale. Buckingham Palace is not like Versailles; it has a domestic character about it, dating back to its origins, and I am not mad about an enormous, out-of-scale vase being plonked in the middle of a lawn. But I shall not complain about it; otherwise they might plonk it down in the middle of Hyde Park.

From memory what is special about Buckingham Palace gardens?

It is the space that is marvellous. At garden parties the Royal Tent is over on one side and the place for refreshments is on the other side. On the left, there are two bandstands in which the Guards' bands play and there are loos, but they are discreetly hidden away. It is a really pleasant experience if the weather is good – which it occasionally is – to walk around in this space, to catch a glimpse of the sovereign and other members of the royal family, to have a cup of tea and enjoy the garden. We British like simple pleasures. We are not Americans who want a great deal of razzmatazz. A nice cup of tea, a glimpse of the Queen, look at the flowers, what could be better?

What do you like about the flowers?

I like herbaceous borders, but I think one of the errors made with them is that there is often too much yellow. I like blues and pinks, and balance. Herbaceous borders of course have their season and it is very important to catch them at the right time, not too early and not too late. I sound almost like Joyce Grenfell, but it is an art to get there at the right moment; so if you are invited to a garden party try and go in the middle of the season rather than right at the beginning or towards the end.

What are your thoughts on the garden façade of the palace?

What I like is the contrast between its exuberance and the quiet dignity of the front. It is highly decorated as is most of Nash's work, and as I live in a Nash house it is not surprising that I like it.

A few, but not many, claim to like Buckingham Palace.

I think the Queen sees it as a place of work really. First and foremost it is the place where she receives ambassadors and ministers, where she reads her boxes and her papers. She is on show there, so for her it is not so much a home as a public place. For her, home is Windsor Castle – that is why the fire there was such a terrible, personal blow for her. She also likes Sandringham, although many people think that architecturally it is inferior. I think it is rather charming but very small of course. I once stayed in the library because all the bedrooms were occupied. She loves Balmoral in Scotland. But she regards Buckingham Palace as a place of work and a place where she is on show to the public whereas I have seen her driving herself through Windsor Great Park alone with no guards. People accept that as quite normal.

What do you see as the role of architecture as far as Buckingham Palace is concerned?

I think that architecture has an extremely important constitutional role. If you look at the Palace of Westminster itself, the Gothic designs of Barry and Pugin are very impressive. It is alive because it was built in the early days of the Gothic revival. Pugin in particular was a genius. The atmosphere he created is that of the importance of the legislature, the dignity of the House of Lords, the important work that is done in the House of Commons; and that is very important. You can add to it and you can, of course, change it. Michael Hopkins has done that excellent building next door for MPs' offices. It has a wonderful central atrium. I am not so sure about the offices because the House of Commons is a place for gossip, not idle gossip but gossip about what is going on in public life. And it is very important, therefore, that you can actually get together in such a place. If you are running from your grand air-conditioned office at the sound of a division bell, avoiding the hovering journalists and different media people, and then running back again, that is not the same. When I first went into the House of Commons all I had was a desk in the cloister, but through having that desk I knew more about what was going on than when I was Leader of the House and had rather nice offices of my own overlooking the river. By being at that desk I saw people, and I learnt what was going on, principally by listening to other people's telephone conversations.

What type of monarchy does the architecture of Buckingham Palace represent?

I think it represents both the very long and very grand history of the country. Entry to it has progressively widened, and it has been added to with the Queen's Gallery and other buildings that have suitable architecture, not totally conformist but architecture that fits in with the main building. But it is the use and the right of entry that are important, and it is the entry that is the great thing that has changed. When I was in politics I spent my life with mayors and when I was chairman of the Royal Fine Art Commission I spent my life with architects. I do not know which was worse: they all have a sense of their own great importance but both are out of touch with ordinary people. As an elected representative of ordinary people one's fingers are on the pulse of the people; one knows what people like. Architects have to be brought back to reality, otherwise they will end up at the top of the tower of Babel and a lot of peoples' lives will be imperilled. And have been in the past.

It has been said that Buckingham Palace is a lumpy piece of Christmas Pudding.

Well, they would say that. You can always look at a building and say it is a this or a that. Do not worry about them.

Some say it is a symbol of empire but we no longer live in an empire.

We live in a post-imperial age. We have only to walk along the streets of our great cities to see how the existence of the empire has determined our population today. It has enriched it but it is also a challenge but not an anachronism. It is there all around us, and if one is to understand our society and why we have it, one has to understand the British Empire.

How do you see Buckingham Palace as a public place?
It is there permanently as part of people's imagination; it is a tool of the imagination by which they can assess the institutions and the life of the country. You do not see a lot of people standing and staring at Westminster Abbey but they know about Westminster Abbey, and they realise that it is the link with an age of faith, which is important but which is no longer with us or at any rate not in that form. Furthermore, people are very busy in London and do not have time to stand and stare. They are rushing about doing things, earning a living; they are trying to catch the next tube train if it has not broken down, or to get on a bus provided there are not five of them all together and then not another one for half an hour. London is a stressful place but I would imagine that one of the good things about retirement is that people will be able to look at things for themselves. But there is a serious point here: the appreciation of architecture requires people not only to look but to see, and they are two different things.

Do you have to stand in front of the palace to know that it is there?
That is one point. But there is the other point that if you want to appreciate architecture, which after all is an art and the most easily accessible of all the arts, all you have to do is to stop and look but having looked you have to see and then you have to make a judgment. The important point is that we have to start in the schools, and we have to teach visual awareness because we are not a visual people.

Do you know Terry Farrell's work?
Yes. I like Terry Farrell very much but I find his work rather over monumental for London.

He has plans to open up the façade of Buckingham Palace with four large arches.
The poor monarchy and the poor Queen who has been on the throne for fifty years and has seen so many crises. To inflict yet another upheaval on her would be really outrageous. And he should not be so silly as to think that that is what is needed at the moment. What is needed for the monarchy is a period of peace. The monarchy has moved forward with the times, and if you have an office, you have to have seclusion. There is also the question today of security and this is very important. When I first went into politics, you used to be able to walk up to the door of 10 Downing Street but you cannot do that anymore. Lady Thatcher put up those appalling gates at the end and you have police barriers too. It is quite ridiculous to think that you can open up to the public indiscriminately a place where the Sovereign of the country and members of her family are. It is just not possible.

Terry Farrell wants to take down the wall.
I think that what Her Majesty wants is a bit of privacy and she likes walking in her garden, as everybody else does. I do not think she would be happy about that. After all, it is not the zoo. It is a combination of an office and a home, and it should be respected as such. This terrible voyeurism of architects is to be deplored, particularly as they all have two central ingredients lacking: they have no imagination and they have no sense of colour.

This institution is ours and we should be able to reach into it as part of the public realm.
I do not think people feel that at all. I think they are very glad to see this impressive piece of architecture. They know that the Queen is working on behalf of the nation inside; they know they will see her on various occasions, and they do not want to feel they own the palace any more than they want people to peer into their own houses. What do English people do when they get a house? They put a fence around it, or they put those Leylandii trees so that they keep everybody out. They want their privacy and I think they accept that the Queen is entitled to hers. But along come these architects and intellectuals and others who really do not understand what people are like, with these mad crazy schemes. Well, away with them! In another age they would have been sent to the Tower!

I N T E R

What do you think of the architecture of Buckingham Palace?

I think that the most disappointing part of Buckingham Palace is the part that you see. Nash's palace is splendid but it is sitting behind the façade. The Aston Webb façade is dull but not as dull as some buildings in London. I thought it was rather hard done by in a recent poll that said it should be demolished. It is typical, worthy Edwardian classicism that complements rather well The Mall and Admiralty Arch at the other end of The Mall. For that reason, and also because it is so widely known and is the defining image of Buckingham Palace, I think it would be wrong to take it down. But it would be wonderful if people could see what is behind.

What idea does it represent in its current form?

I think Buckingham Palace represents an architectural relic of imperialism. There is no doubt that it is immensely pompous. **It is essentially a stage set that actually looks like what it is: a façade stuck on another building** The Aston Webb façade is essentially a stage set that actually looks like what it is: a façade stuck on another building. It stands behind this great forecourt, which has rather oddly dressed soldiers marching up and down it, unnecessarily, for the tourists; and then there is this area outside the railings slightly fenced off, with the faces of tourists pressed against it as if in a cage; but you are never quite sure whether it is the tourists in the cage or the monarch in the cage. The whole thing is very old fashioned but that is the point. I think it is slightly ridiculous to say that because we have a modern monarchy it should be located in a flat. Part of the point of the British monarchy is its continuity, its history. The bit of London that is about monarchy is the bit that goes from The Mall to Buckingham Palace, the processional route.

Is the architecture itself fitting for that?

The point about Buckingham Palace is that it is at the end of a processional route along The Mall from Admiralty Arch. There are not many processional routes in London in the great classical beaux-arts tradition. This is the one we have; it is where coaches ride up and down with horses in front of them, and members of the public stand and cheer. It is very difficult to do that in Cheapside or the Strand or Oxford Street. The Mall is where we can find so to speak our processions.

Buckingham Palace is a part of the stage set of that processional route. That is something quite different from what I would do with Buckingham Palace. As far as that is concerned, having established that it is the building at the end of the processional route – the backdrop to the stage if you like –I think that the building itself is so wonderful inside that the public ought to be able to see it much more easily than they can at the moment; and there are all kinds of things that I would do with Buckingham Palace behind that façade that would not damage the façade.

Do you think that the institution of monarchy should become more transparent?

I am very suspicious of architects who say make it transparent by making it glass. The transparency of Buckingham Palace will come from people being able to get round the back. It is as simple as that. It may be inconvenient for the monarch, or for

SIMON JENKINS

V I E W S

palace staff but it works elsewhere and there is no reason why the palace should not feel as accessible as, for instance, Windsor Castle. In many ways Windsor Castle is far more of a residence than Buckingham Palace. Windsor Castle is one of the most magnificent palaces in Europe and is to my mind wholly accessible in feel. When you go round Windsor Castle although a lot of it is not open to the public you feel as if you have seen the palace. I really do not see why that should not be possible at Buckingham Palace. I think it could be used far more to open up the monarchy.

There is no good exhibition of monarchy in Britain; there is nowhere you get a sense of the continuity of history, the traditions of the monarchy, the headship of State. The obvious place to put it is in Buckingham Palace or in one of the other attendant palaces, in St James's perhaps.

Why should you feel that you cannot look into the palace?
I do not think the Queen wants it. It is as simple as that. It is her palace; it is her building; she is quite resistant to access and I think that as long as she is in charge you are very unlikely to get any movement. I am given to understand that she has been quite enthusiastic about a wider opening in the Jubilee Year. She has agreed to open the palace gardens much more extensively. These are all good things. I think that naturally she is a conservative person, and she does not like her property to be subject to what is after all a huge tourist intrusion. She does not want Buckingham Palace being more penetrated than it is now. Either way, it is her palace at the same time as being paid for by the State. So I think that a debate should take place between the monarch and the State about the appropriate use of the palace.

I also have to say that if anybody is concerned about the longevity of the monarchy, about the stability of the monarchy, about the popularity of the monarchy – and all these things are legitimate concerns – the manner in which the **It is her palace; it is her building; she is quite resistant to access** monarch makes his or her buildings available to the public is part and parcel of that. Buckingham Palace – and indeed other royal palaces in London – are very inaccessible places. They have very big walls around them; they have huge security. The security, I think, is often overdone and tends to exist even when they are not resident in the buildings. An awful lot could be done if there was a will.

What do you think of the walls that surround the gardens?
I think the walls are a pity. They are very high, unattractive walls, with big skips on them and barbed wire and electronic devices. They are offputting, alienating, hostile. I do not think the monarchy wants that in this day and age. The gardens of Buckingham Palace are very little used; so much so that they are regarded as an important nature reserve. I think that to take down the walls and to put up railings or whatever you could substitute for them would be a huge asset in terms of visual accessibility. It has to be said this is a very precious bit of open space in central London and I have always thought the obvious thing to do in the long-term was to treat the gardens of Buckingham Palace and the gardens of Lancaster House and St James's Palace as part of a semi-public extension of Green Park and St James's Park. Some of the walls could be

eliminated; some I know are historic but they do make the area seem very hostile and alien and to see very large numbers of tourists who have come to see London and admire our monarchical institutions wandering bleakly past these great high walls is a depressing sight. There is no good reason why some buildings should not be more accessible; there are three or four of them that are just shut up most of the time. It is quite wrong.

The eight-foot high walls around the monarch's garden in Central London block my view?

Well the way you put the question I agree with you. I think it should be perfectly possible to replace these walls with fences so that you can see through to the west front of Buckingham Palace. It is very fine architecture Nash's west front. Frankly there is no reason why people should not walk through those gardens and get into the palace that way. It cannot be beyond the wit of security to protect the building and its inhabitants from the public. Even without a police state these things are feasible if there is a will to succeed. In most palaces in Europe there is the will, and it has been done; there is no reason why it should not be done in the centre of London in one of the great homes of monarchy, where people are proud of their monarch. I think the monarchy could make an effort to be more visually accessible than it is now.

[The walls] are off-putting, alienating, hostile, I don't think the Monarchy wants that in this day and age

What does that say about the way the monarchy relates to the people?

Not much, frankly. I do not think it is a big issue. I think that the fact that Buckingham Palace is a rather cold, slightly awesome, slightly deterring place surrounded by immense security does not mean anything except that we are security mad in this country. We have done the same to Downing Street. We used to be able to drive up to the door of Downing Street. I could show tourists where my Prime Minister lived from the window of my car but I cannot do that any more. And I cannot do it at Buckingham Palace either. I think that there needs to be one big push to open up these buildings a bit more. I do not think that architecture of a certain sort adds to the mystique of monarchy or to the feeling of lofty authority of the monarchy. People do not see monarchs that way. They see the monarch through the media, through photographs, through television, through where she goes, where she performs; that is what matters to the monarchy. I see a very beautiful building. I see three or four beautiful buildings and lovely gardens and parks; they are a part of the city that I paid for and I think that I ought to be able to see more of them, that they should be more accessible.

Who owns the palace? Are Buckingham Palace and its gardens mine?

Buckingham Palace belongs to the State; it is held by the State; it is paid for by the State; and it is owned by the State as the principal residence for the Head of State. There is no arguing about that. The taxpayer pays for Buckingham Palace; the taxpayer keeps up the gardens. The tradition is that they are the permanent residence of the monarch, and the monarch therefore says what happens to them as a long-term tenant would normally do. But they do belong to the State and we are a democracy. They are not like Sandringham, which is the private property of the monarch.

Should I have a voice about how I would like the palace to change?

Well, that is complete nonsense. The royal palaces come under the Royal Palaces Agency. They are paid for by the Exchequer out of tax revenue. On the other hand, the permanent tenant is the monarch who, like all permanent tenants, has pretty free reign over the properties. If you are taking out a 99-year lease or a 999-year lease on a property, while the landlord or the freeholder would retain some rights, I think the general view is that you can do more or less what you like with the property and that is the view that successive monarchs and successive governments have taken. However, it is paid for on a running basis by the State so it is different from a straightforward lease; we pay money every year for the staff at Buckingham Palace. I think the situation is that there is a relationship of consent between the monarchy and the government over the proper management of Buckingham Palace. It was a matter of discussion when the palace was opened to the public. It was apparently opened to pay for the repairs to Windsor Castle after the great fire there. I think everybody regarded that as a good thing. The palace had resisted until then, but once it had opened after the great fire, the palace has accepted that it remain open a little longer each year. We have our foot in the door and we are pushing it further every year. It is a pity that it is not open slightly more welcomingly and wider. I sense this will happen. The public paid for that place. It is not the Queen's private property like Sandringham, and I think to that extent although I would respect the desire of a very public person for privacy, and that privacy has to be respected, there are plenty of private parts of Buckingham Palace and the Queen has plenty of other palaces and so she is not without places where she can find privacy.

Buckingham Palace is a rather cold, slightly awesome, slightly deterring place surrounded by immense security

Buckingham Palace is in the centre of London. It is a major tourist attraction and it is a State-owned building. I think it should be more widely accessible.

Only on very rare occasions is the palace the focus of public events.
Buckingham Palace is the bit of London that is about the monarch. I like to see London in bits: the City is about money; Parliament Square is about politics; Trafalgar Square is about the old empire; Piccadilly Circus is about entertainment; Oxford Circus is about retail. London has these quartiers; the royal quartier is around the Victoria monument, at the end of The Mall. If it lacks a certain emotional focus in other aspects of national life that is because it is about the monarch. Nowadays the monarchy is not immensely important in British politics or commerce but the monarch is the Head of State and therefore you go to the Victoria Memorial, you go and stand in front of Buckingham Palace when there is a royal occasion but not on other occasions. For instance, military occasions are not celebrated there any more. To that extent Buckingham Palace, St James's Palace, Lancaster House, Marlborough House, Clarence House form the royal quartier of London. They are like the Louvre used to be in Paris in the old days. I do not think they are exploited as such and I do not think people feel about all those buildings as they might. If I was marketing the monarchy I would make far more of this physical presence in the centre of the capital. They are actually in a backwater, mostly inhabited by tourists during the day and uninhabited by the royals much of the time. It is a part of London that is used in the season in the old-fashioned sense, and I just think somebody should take a grip on it and say, "Come on now, these are beautiful buildings, this is a lovely part of town, there are parks and gardens all around it, and it really could be made more exciting and more informative of the concept of the monarchy."

You have a monarch who is not essentially a Londoner, who does not identify with the capital and I think does not like London very much

The palace is neglected. Is this the psyche of the modern monarchy?
There are two points: one is that you have at the moment a monarch who is not essentially a Londoner, who does not identify with the capital and I think does not like London very much. She prefers to be in the country or in Windsor, and so you do not feel that bond between monarch and city that you felt with some monarchs in the past – although I have to say not many. Secondly, and much more important, I think that of late the advisors to the monarch have simply felt very hesitant, very vulnerable, about the monarchy and they are terrified of making or suggesting any changes that might damage what might be called the mystique. There is a fear that if you make the monarch more accessible, if you make the concept of monarchy more marketable, if you introduce new concepts, or if you simply open it up a bit more, you might start destroying it. Timidity is one of the reasons it has proved so difficult to get the public into Buckingham Palace at all. Almost every other monarch in British history has given gardens to the London public. It is only recently that the monarch has been unable to hand over any more territory to the public. It is almost as if they are trying to claw it back: the Crown Estate is building housing estates in Regent's Park. That is outrageous and wrong.

Is the way The Mall and Buckingham Palace are configured relevant in a post-imperial age?
Yes, for two reasons. One is that every country has ceremonial, has a Head of State, has rituals associated with the headship of State. Countries that do not have processional routes get in a bit of a mess about it. The Trooping of the Colour, the State Opening of Parliament need straight lines, coaches, horses, cheering crowds. It does not have much to do with empire; these are simply the appurtenances of any state. We have them and they happen to date from when we had an empire, but that is neither here nor there. We are rather lucky to the extent that we have these splendid buildings and we can show them off regularly. Every generation makes a few changes: the uniforms have become slightly less pompous; the ritual slightly less ethereal; but most members of the public, and this is the ultimate test, like the fact that they have this ritual, like the fact that there is a processional route and that the year is punctuated by these royal occasions. So I think the task is to try and keep everything reasonably up to date, and to ask fairly regularly if there are ways we could do things better if only to protect the monarchy.

They are terrified of making or suggesting any changes that might damage what might be called the mystique

Do you feel strongly about this when you walk down The Mall?
You need to remember why it is where it is. It was the hunting ground originally and it was wild open country but the houses in St James's put up walls to protect their gardens from the rabble outside. Now you have to understand that that particular form of conversation is precious. I feel very strongly about conserving palaces. I find them beautiful, full of lovely things and

a pleasure to go round. I feel strongly about walls and I think that these walls that were built to keep people out detract from the beauty of the park. The Mall is a road but it is also a promenade. It has always been a promenade. Now it is very crowded and a very popular place with visitors to London. The way in which it is configured on the Pall Mall side is interesting: there is the absolutely splendid undercroft of Carlton House Terrace, then when you get to the earlier eighteenth and seventeenth century palaces you come to these walls, which prevent you seeing more gardens which you should be allowed to see. At Kensington Palace you can see the gardens through the railings; why not those of Marlborough House, or Lancaster House, or St James's Palace? You do not feel that you are a part of these buildings and you do not feel that they are a part of the city. As part and parcel of making these buildings more accessible, their gardens should also be more accessible.

At Kensington Palace you can see the gardens through the railings; why not those of Lancaster House, or St James's Palace?

Do you know Terry Farrell?
Yes.

What do you think of Terry Farrell's architecture?
I think Terry Farrell is a master London architect. I like particularly some of his infilling work. My favourite, the Comyn Ching Triangle in Covent Garden, is one of the best examples of how to place new buildings in the context of old buildings. I think his particular talent is in taking the historical idiom of London, which for the most part is Georgian but not exclusively so, and fitting it into the spaces in between existing buildings. And that is why I would be interested to know what he wants to do with Buckingham Palace.

What would you do with Buckingham Palace?
I think the building that Nash built, which is still there behind, is a much more exciting building in every way than the one we have now. It had wings reaching out towards you; it had that baroque effect that you get from that sort of architecture. You could see in the portico an entrance. You had a sense of both privacy and closure but also openness. It was a much more successful building than the Blore wing, the east wing, that was put across the front to provide more rooms so that when Ottoman emperors came to visit Queen Victoria their retinues could be put up. Those days are now over and the rooms mostly unused. There is no need for that wing really and so it could be taken down. However, I have to say that of all the acts of demolition that I would like to do in London this has to be pretty low on my list of priorities. And since it is very, very unlikely to happen, it is a somewhat academic discussion as to whether it would be a good idea to replace it with something else. If you were to alter it I would remove it and put back in effect the Nash building. I think that messing about with the east wing façade is a waste of discussion time let alone a waste of money.

Is The Mall processional route now antiquated and should it be replaced by a public square?
Yes. Most squares it has to be said are surrounded by buildings and they are used by people in a multitude of different ways. A courtyard in front of the palace is slightly different. How much more would you get out of making Buckingham Palace more like Versailles, or the other great urban palaces of Europe? I am not sure.

You could do things with Buckingham Palace. It is not one of the world's great buildings. Even if you were to remove the east wing facade or the Blore wing you have got frankly just another large grand house. It is not a part of the urban fabric in the way it would be if it was off Trafalgar Square, or Piccadilly Circus, or Piccadilly. It is out on its own, a building of a certain sort in a certain place. I can see that you could get more people in front by clearing the traffic around the Victoria Monument but I do not see much purpose in bringing the railings closer to the house.

The forecourt is pretty pointless at the moment, except for the Changing of the Guard but that is one of the most popular tourist events in Europe so you would be losing something if you could not change the guard behind a reasonably secure barrier of some sort. But these are technicalities. As I said, I am much more concerned about the high walls that surround the gardens.

Are you in favour of changing the forecourt?
No. It is a ceremonial space. It has always been used for ceremonial, for parades, for visiting heads of state to be greeted reasonably protected from the crowd. It serves its purpose.

Should there be more openings in the west front?
There is a very good parallel for what I would do with the garden of Buckingham Palace. It is Queen Mary's Garden in Regent's Park. This was a private garden: it belonged to the Royal Botanic Society until 1932 and was their private club garden. They could not make a go of it and the lease came to an end in 1932. Queen Mary, who was a very determined lady, seized it and said she would give it to the people of London. It was integrated into Regent's Park but behind closeable railings. You pay to get in and it can be locked. It is an ornamental garden as is the Buckingham Palace garden. I think you should be able to go in and out of the palace garden quite freely and it should be a part of Green Park and St James's Park just as Queen Mary's Garden is part of Regent's Park. It would be different because it is laid out differently and needs very careful tending and looking after. It probably also needs resting occasionally but there is no reason why it should not be open to the public. If Queen Mary's Garden can be open to the public so can the gardens of Buckingham Palace.

Is there a legitimate reason now to readdress the urban design of Buckingham Palace?
There is a case for simply saying, "How can this building fit into the West End of London and the tourist quarter of London more sympathetically, in less hostile fashion?" I am less concerned with its appearance. It is a historic building; it has become accepted in its present shape, form and appearance, and I would be very reluctant to change that. I am simply conservative to that degree.

But is it an acknowledgment of the history of the monarchy rather than of the monarchy as a living, active institution of the State?
Yes, to the latter; no to the first. I do think the monarchy is the peculiar way in which we have ourselves a Head of State. It is a historical phenomenon. It is impossible to separate the hereditary monarchy of Britain from our history, which is what heredity is all about. Press it too hard and it begins to implode. You have to respect its history or you cannot respect Britain. I feel that very strongly. I support it. It is preferable to the alternatives. That is as far as I would go. It does need supporting and therefore in some sense it needs to be protected, and it needs to be worried about. In other words, if it is unpopular it is in big trouble, so it needs to be kept popular. The role played in that popularity by the buildings is very, very much a subsidiary issue. I would make the existing buildings more accessible. I would make sure that there are regular bonuses given to the pubic insofar as that is within the Queen's power. One of these is the gardens, the other the accessibility of the palaces. However, these are not essential to the preservation of the monarchy. They are just things that I think would be rather nice if they could find their way to doing them.

How can this building fit into the West End of London in a less hostile fashion?

Why can't they find their way to doing them?
I think there is more than just deep conservatism there because the monarchy has shown itself able to change. I think there is a deep nervousness, which is quite different, about making gestures that might expose the monarchy to question. I think that is very short-sighted. It is a reasonably robust institution, a reasonably popular institution, and it could afford to exploit its assets more vigorously than it does at present.

I N T E R

Do you like the architecture of Buckingham Palace as it stands now?

Buckingham Palace is basically an eighteenth century palace, done as wallpaper by Aston Webb in 1913. It was built at night in three months and it looks it, as many people have said. This is fast-food architecture; it is a kind of Hollywood stage set, not serious high classicism. It is a façade put on a previously existing building that had started to crumble. It is pompous and is not the right symbol for the monarchy today: it is imperial. It is not even British in a way, more French or German. I do not like it as architecture; it is inferior architecture.

Why are people curious about Buckingham Palace?

People go to Buckingham Palace the way they go to the World Trade Centre after September 11. They go with great

This is fast-food architecture, it is a kind of Hollywood stage set

expectations of emotion, of experiencing a relationship with the monarch and the nation. Tourists do not see a building; they see the images in their minds of a fairytale palace. We are so used to seeing it on television, particularly when the royal family come out on the balcony on royal occasions such as marriages, that it has become a backdrop, a stage set that has no meaning. And so it is lodged in people's minds the way it is and to change it at all would be to transgress the way people think of it and that would make them very angry indeed, understandably so because that is how such symbols work. If you redesigned St Peter's in Rome, Catholics would be outraged. Of course it has been redesigned over a thousand years and one has to redesign and so go through this crucible of raising questions, having a natural reaction and then asking how we deal with the symbols because the role of monarchy in the end is symbolic. The Queen may talk about 'my government' and it may be known as 'Her Majesty's Government' but everybody in Britain knows that she has no power except the power to consult. In raising the question of the palace you are asking what should be the symbolism of the

Tourists do not see a building; they see the images in their minds of a fairytale palace

monarchy for the twenty-first century. That is the key issue and clearly what we have is something that was designed and built in 1901 at the end of the high period of empire, of imperial war, and I am sure that that is not what either the monarchy or the people want the monarchy to symbolise today. Magic and mystery were the foundation of the monarchy in the nineteenth century. Bagehot wrote in 1867, "Don't let any daylight on monarchy or it will lose its magic." Well, since 1969 floodlights have been trained on the royal family and it has lost that sense of magic.

Is Buckingham Palace an anachronism?

It is in terms of where the monarchy should be going in the twenty-first century.

You once compared Buckingham Palace to a Hollywood home. What did you mean?

In Hollywood, they sell maps of where the movie stars live. You can buy them and tour round their homes, which are a mixture of a classical palace and an understated back-home American house. The movie star house has a very peculiar relationship with the public because movie stars want desperately to be looked at and at the same time to disappear

CHARLES JENCKS

V I E W S

because they want to lead a private life while still wanting to be the most famous movie star on the block. So they send out a double signal: look at me and do not look at me. The architecture that results is unobtrusive in the extreme. In other words everything has been taken away and then put back as classical clichés and so it becomes a pastiche. It is neither one thing nor the other but has the worst of both worlds and I think that that is what somebody has done to Buckingham Palace: it was designed as something that should not be there and should be there. The architecture is very heavy, dramatic, eighteenth-century architecture and yet at the same time understated and unobtrusive in the extreme.

So monarchy is about symbolism and Buckingham Palace is the symbol of the power of the monarchy?
There is an argument that the palace should disappear and that the monarchy should be in the background as a rock of conservatism in a sea of fast change. You do not want it in the foreground; you do not want it to speak out on issues. You want it to say nothing and thus symbolise that things will never change. But in fact as we know the monarch has no power, except the power of the media and this is different from the kind of power conveyed by their architecture. When the monarchy displays its power the whole system is dressed in neogothic: people wear ermine; they wear wigs; they behave as if they were in a charade; they ride on horseback and in carriages. This ritual is fine on certain occasions, say marriages, but it should have a different edge today and this is particularly true of the royal parks and palaces.

What should the architecture of Buckingham Palace represent?
There is no reason to redesign it from scratch because it is not falling down and you should not change things just for the sake of bringing them up to date. It is important that any change should come from a new function and this new function really is the role of the monarch going directly to the people. That is the important shift that Prince Charles tried to introduce with his stands on health, on organic farming, and on community architecture. They were attempts to get round the bureaucracy, the elite, the aristocracy and the powerbrokers and to go direct to the people. That is the role of the monarchy; the Prince knows that. When he was at Cambridge he studied thirteenth-century monarchy, and he made that famous remark: "Of course the monarchy is an elective institution: if the people don't want us they won't have us; they will get rid of us." That is an extraordinarily radical statement. It is radical because he understood this link between monarchy and the people. It is a direct link, a radical link that is now mediated through the media, especially television. If we have a television monarchy, then let the monarch go directly to the people and let Buckingham Palace be a beacon.

You should not change things just for the sake of bringing them up to date

Does the current building speak to us as a people?
If you drive around Buckingham Palace and its gardens and you look at the different buildings, what you see most of the time is keep out signs, high walls and barbed wire. These things are very aggressive, and alienate the monarch from the people. It is as if they were at war. Or else you see a very uptight façade that says nothing. The message is all to do with

control and there is nothing enjoyable about it. It is as if being a monarch was a real pain. And dangerous! There is none of the magic that Bagehot asked for in the nineteenth century. Being a monarch cannot always be a burden. It should be a celebration.

What do you mean by a 'keep-out mentality'?

The 'keep out mentality' just grows historically. I do not think there is anything more to it than that. If you have a big palace and a big estate you ring fence it, especially in a major city where there is the possibility of revolution, or conflict, or murder. It is not at all surprising that all these things exist; it is just that they do not have to exist in the same way today. There is also the complicated relationship between a private residence, which it is, and its public function. And those two aspects get mixed up in the wrong way. If you can divide the two as they do in some country houses that are open to the public, then the public can enjoy their part of it and the privates lives of the owners are not disturbed. Their private life must be private, must not be invaded, and must be totally secure. It is just that we have today inherited the wrong relationship between the two systems, so that the private symbols say 'keep out' and that sign predominates whereas today we can protect the monarch in other ways and separate those functions, as is done in other countries where royal palaces are much more enjoyed and much more used.

Redesigning the palace would lead to a reconsideration of the monarchy's role

Should the forecourt be used as a public place?

The difficulties in redesigning it are great. One should not underrate it because after all people go there to be given titles. There are larger semi-public, semi-private, highly controlled theatrical events that occur throughout the year, which would have to be redesigned in a different place. I can see that the royal family would be upset by having it redesigned because why change what they are used to? And yet they genuinely want to re-negotiate their role with the media and with the country and are always looking for new ways to do this. Redesigning the palace would lead to a reconsideration of their role.

They do not want the forecourt to be a public space?

I am sure they want to keep Buckingham Palace as private as they possibly can, for good reason. So much of their life is invaded already. There is the fear of the people getting out of control; there is a fear of assassination and anthrax in everybody's mind. But that is not a reason not to reconsider a way around it because you can make things safe and redesign them too. Why should they want to live in outmoded dress? It is like speaking in sixteenth century words. I do not say "Prithee, kind sir, may I take thy coat?" You feel absurd acting in the wrong century all the time so there must be ways in which they themselves want to change the style of their life, ways which none of us can imagine. But they also want to renegotiate their relationship with the media and with the people of Britain so it is a case of sitting down at the table and working out the right way of putting Humpty Dumpty together again.

Is it absurd that we are having this conversation?

The role of government is being renegotiated in these kinds of conversation in Washington DC, in New Delhi, and around the world. The symbols of the Jefferson Monument, the Lincoln Memorial, and the White House are rather trite today. They are pompous, nineteenth-century classical style things that are an embarrassment. They are almost as bad as Stalin's architecture. You always have to renew your symbols to give them new life, to make them credible. If they lose their credibility the people will take them over. The Lincoln Memorial is an interesting example. Until the early 1960s there was no place for people to congregate and then, because of the civil rights movement, Martin Luther King and a million people took it over and from then on it became like Trafalgar Square, which has also been taken over by the people, renewed and given new life. That is the role of the people in a democracy. It is a dynamic process; they take possession of space, and renegotiate the symbols. Now the Lincoln Memorial, like Buckingham Palace is just a backdrop for what occurs on its steps. You do not necessarily have to redesign it in a different style. New events lead to the situation where people ask what the monarchy means to them in the twenty-first century. It is a key question because of the media power of monarchy. If we were in the nineteenth century and the English constitution was still the way it was then you could say that it did not need to be renegotiated. But it is clear that it is not working in the right way. If you have a monarchy it is necessary to make it work in the best possible way. In a sense on a functional level it is a glorified ombudsman that takes popular stands on politically unpopular lines. It stands up for the people against the bureaucrats, the politicians. It innovates; it gives strength in times of catastrophe. I am, of course, able to say this as an American who has nothing to gain or to lose from it. I have no feelings one way or the other. I am not anti- or pro-monarchist. But I do believe that if you have a monarchy it could be made to work better. And so it is a very important discussion.

Does the Changing of the Guard serve a purpose?
Clearly the whole panoply of monarchy and the ritual of the State Opening of Parliament, royal weddings and State occasions go together as a single package with the palaces. It is all part of the neogothic style of government. And so people want it to remain because it symbolises the continuity of the British nation. And it gives them great consolation in times of hardship. They fought the Second World War to keep that system going. It is a form of magic that particularly expresses itself at royal weddings and funerals that are beamed around the world to one or perhaps two billion people. So it is not only the British who have that view. People do not really want to change anything because the British do it so well.

Does Buckingham Palace fit into the ideal of magic?
The palace plays a role but it is a bland background of second-rate architecture that could be made to work a lot better.

Do you like Terry Farrell's work?
I like a lot of Terry's work because he is an urbanist above all. He thinks about putting together different opportunities that are real: how people work, streets, squares, parks, nature. Urbanism is a complex art because to control all that you have to be wise about economic things; you have to persuade people all the time; you have to gather consent. It is a highly political kind of design and I think Terry does that better than any other architect with the possible exception of Richard Rogers, who is also very urbanistically inclined. In the past his architecture *per se* – like the high security MI6 building – tended to be fun.

What about the new arches he is proposing through the east front of the Palace?
I would have to see how the whole design fits together but remember that the original design was part of a long imperial presentation scheme, and you would have to redesign that so that it would be less of a fantasy and would work better. I think that opening up Buckingham Palace to the park system is a very interesting idea. We could have water gardens in the gardens of Buckingham Palace and its picture collection could be dramatised. It has one of the greatest art collections in the world and that could be made much more accessible and public and open.

Should the forecourt to the Palace be a public square?
When you say a square, you mean a place for people to come and congregate; you do not mean restaurants or hot dog stalls? Perhaps something like the forecourt of the Louvre or Siena would possibly be a good idea. Obviously people would not live there and commercial activity would be at a minimum but the idea of being able to go in there, have a coffee and take possession of it for the people would be a very positive idea and would not necessarily compromise the private lives or security of the Royal Family. So yes, it is a good idea. It is very sad the way that tourists now press their faces to the railings. You know that the lord is in his castle and the servant at the gate. That is not the right way to relate to people any more. I think it could be done with style, with much more enjoyment.

You know the lord is in his castle and the servant at the gate

Should we risk tinkering with such places?
It would be a very high risk for a politician to say anything about the monarchy but it is different for an architect. There is still some risk because people do not want to tinker with the monarchy at all, and there will be a flurry of excitement and tut tuts. But opening a discussion is positive and a bit of anger that stirs up the pot is no bad thing.

As a full-frontal attack on the palace it could be perceived as radical but since it has no political or even social agenda beyond letting the people be more accessible to the monarch and vice versa, then there is nothing subversive about it. It is neither left wing nor right wing. It is not a real threat. The only threat is to style and symbol. But of course there are people who will say that it is outrageous to even think of messing with a great symbol of our past.

And should Terry be sent to the Tower?
I thought we lived in democracy!

Conclusion

Above: The Jubilee celebrations, which included a pop concert, marked a rare display of allegiance between the monarchy and the people
Left: Laser displays and fireworks illuminate the Buckingham Palace as the million-strong crowd celebrates the Queen's Jubilee in June 2002

The primary motivation for drawing up these concepts was my long-held belief that the royal parks and palaces are London's primary public realm and virtually the only world-class public realm in the urban metropolis of this great capital city.

The work so far has been a reconnaissance exercise. What does this major piece of the public realm mean to us as British people, as Londoners? How can it be better used? We will not find out what is needed without questioning very slowly, one step at a time, what Buckingham Palace represents for us. I have found that you cannot question in the abstract. You have to put an idea on the table and say 'what if'? I would like to be an advance party for the possible. Perhaps the right answer is much bolder than my proposals. But we shall not find it without asking questions. I do not believe in sitting back and keeping quiet out of pure politeness. Below is a summary of my thoughts so far.

An urbanist should stimulate society by making suggestions for improvements that reflect what we are and where we think we are going. I am trying to readdress the relationship of our parks and palaces so that they better express the reality of our time and we all benefit more from them.

Manifesting the theatre of life in our urban spaces is what urban design is all about. But at Buckingham Palace and in the parks we have erected barriers and have not fulfilled their potential. The barriers have diminished our great set pieces. My aim is to put back meaning and opportunity.

Nash's great courtyard originally enabled Buckingham Palace to open its arms and symbolise a great home. Once Aston Webb's screen was added, a Victorian vision of monarchy appeared and the palace represented a colonising institution. The resulting complex is neither neighbourly nor good design. It does nothing for the royal parks or the public realm. It is far too grand and triumphalist. It sells us the idea of anti-communication – hardly the right concept for today.

The palace complex is the public's front room, the main square of Britain. It is the place for great ceremonies: weddings, victory celebrations and funerals. Yet it needs a greater sense of purpose. The public and pedestrians should have a clear run of the place and must be allowed nearer. When the royal coach approaches or the royal family comes out onto the balcony, people rush to the railings. We are made to feel like paupers at the gate. Like giants and mice. It is promoting the wrong kind of relationship.

It is the urban setting that tells you that this is Buckingham Palace, not the actual building itself. All the ingredients for urban theatre are there: the big circle, the gates (which, by the way, do not lead anywhere), the suburban lawn and the sweeping traffic. Is it a roundabout? Is it part of the London road system? Or is it a pedestrian space? This nameless place cannot make up its mind what it is, which is why it fails. It could be much more successful but the theatre is played out without the full involvement of the British public. To watch the Horse Guards among a clutter of traffic is very strange. No one seems to have thought through what it means, yet for most people it is the most important public space in Britain.

Our idea is to put giant openings in the front to create a grand entrance, rather like Nash's Marble Arch – which at one time fronted the palace. This would enable penetration through to the courtyard beyond. The famous wedding cake façade would become a gateway, a symbol of openness.

We all know that the royal family lives away from the palace for a lot of the time and the private apartments take up a single wing: the rest is public rooms. We cannot enjoy the splendours of the palace and gardens in the way their designers, builders and creators intended. It is a loss that we could rediscover without having to turn our backs on tradition. If it were all opened up, we would discover great riches found in no other city in the world. The ceremony would continue but there would be something for the future too.

I would like to take the best of it all, develop it without throwing it away, penetrate through that screen, create a public space and make it all work with additions and reinterpretations that would retain the best of history. I think that would be sublime.

*Above: Aerial showing the palace as an impenetrable
island surrounded by the crowds.*

Below: Views of the post-celebration clear up. The infrastructure is clearly inadequate and the surrounding area is left as a tawdry mess – a significant contrast to the grandiosity of the actual celebrations.